JUN - 2003

THE COUNTRY
GARDEN

THE COUNTRY GARDEN

*How to Plan and Plant a
Garden That Grows Itself*

CHARLIE RYRIE

Reader's
Digest

A READER'S DIGEST BOOK

This edition published by The Reader's Digest Association by arrangement with
Collins & Brown

FOR COLLINS & BROWN
Project Editor: Gillian Haslam
Copy Editor: Maggi McCormick
Designer: Anne Wilson
Illustrator: Kate Simunek
Picture Researcher: Louise Daubeny

FOR READER'S DIGEST
U.S. Project Editor: Miranda Smith
Canadian Project Editor: Pamela Johnson
Project Designer: George McKeon
Executive Editor, Trade Publishing: Dolores York
Senior Design Director: Elizabeth Tunnicliffe
Director, Trade Publishing: Christopher T. Reggio
Vice President & Publisher, Trade Publishing: Harold Clarke

NOTE TO OUR READERS
This publication contains the opinions and ideas of its author and is designed to
provide useful information to the reader. It is not intended as a substitute for the
advice of an expert on the subject matter covered. Products or active ingredients,
treatments, and the names of organizations which appear in this publication are
included for informational purposes only; the inclusion of commercial products in the
book does not imply endorsement by Reader's Digest, nor does the omission of any
product or active ingredient or treatment advice indicate disapproval by Reader's
Digest. When using any commercial product, readers should read and follow all
label directions carefully.

The author and publisher specifically disclaim any responsibility for any liability,
loss, or risk (personal, financial, or otherwise) that may be claimed or incurred as
a consequence—directly or indirectly—of the use and/or application of any of the
contents of this publication.

Library of Congress Cataloging in Publication Data

Ryrie, Charlie.
   The country garden : how to plan and plant a garden that grows itself / by
Charlie Ryrie.
      p. cm.
   ISBN 0-7621-0391-4
   1. Landscape gardening. 2. Gardening. I. Title.

SB473 .R97 2003
635–dc21   2002067907

Address any comments about *The Country Garden* to:
   The Reader's Digest Association, Inc.
   Adult Trade Publishing
   Reader's Digest Road
   Pleasantville, NY 10570-7000

For Reader's Digest products and information, visit our website:
   www.rd.com (in the United States)
   www.readersdigest.ca (in Canada)

Printed and bound in Malaysia by Times Offset (M) Sdn. Bhd

1 3 5 7 9 10 8 6 4 2

Contents

Introduction

It is difficult to define a country garden, as they vary so much in the hands of different gardeners, but all are unpretentious and unselfconscious. It may be full of traditional favorites like tall hollyhocks and spired delphiniums with roses around the door, but it needn't be old-fashioned. It may have formal elements, but it will be informal. It may be tidy, but it should never be restrained. The best are relaxed affairs, looking as though they have evolved naturally — with just a little help from the gardeners.

A country garden should be a living, working garden, containing vegetables, herbs, and fruit if possible, plus as many flowers as can fit into the available space. These flowers should mingle in a riot of color and scent, spilling into and falling over each other in beds and pots, up walls, along fences. One great thing about this style of gardening is that there are no rules, and another huge advantage is that your garden should largely take care of itself once you have the basics sorted out. This is where we can take cues from the earliest country gardeners who were short of time, money, and space, yet still created productive and increasingly beautiful gardens over the centuries.

Left: An idyllic spot to relax in this unpretentious garden, where favorite flowers spread through the profusion of roses in a happy jumble.

Right: Old-fashioned roses are hallmarks of any country garden, along boundaries, in borders, or scrambling up walls or trees.

The country garden heritage

The very first country gardens came into being in Britain in the 14th century following the Black Death and a forced reorganization of labor, which created the first rural tenants with dwellings and patches of land they could call their own. Subsistence was what mattered, so country gardeners grew predominantly turnips and cabbages to supplement beans and wheat grown in the fields, simply because the tenants could just about survive on them. These grew alongside a few potherbs and flowers invited in from the wild because they had curative properties — for example violets, lady's mantle, yarrow, monkshood, bellflowers, tansy, betony, and columbine. Country garden plants have always been easy to care for and propagate, and most garden favorites spread by self-seeding prolifically or growing into generous clumps that are easy to divide and share. Primroses, cowslips, and periwinkles made early appearances, with honeysuckle, briar rose, cranesbill, foxglove, mulleins, cornflowers, corn marigolds, and campions not far behind. Many of these original flowers are still welcomed eagerly, though today's varieties are more sophisticated than the original wildings.

The earliest country gardens were a bit of a jumble, with the greater part of the space devoted to vegetables and herbs, with other flowers mixed in at random. Fowl usually roamed freely, and a pig was kept in a small enclosure. The muck from the domestic animals and the household was used on the garden, along with the slops, so the soil became rich and productive. No self-respecting cottage garden today should

The jeweled colors of alliums, iris, and peonies dominate this early summer bed, complementing the pale flowers of veronica and tobacco plants and the dark green, silver, and bronze foliage plants.

be without its compost heap, even if you don't keep animals to produce your own manure.

Sweetly scented plants were always important for disguising the odors of day-to-day living, and Madonna lilies crept into cottage gardens very early on, gleaned from the monks and nuns who kept the monastic physic gardens that contained flowering plants for scent and strewing as well as ornament. To this day, the lilies seem to grow best in sunny borders in humbler gardens rather than in more

formal situations. As early as the 16th century most country gardens boasted an apple tree, often a pear and sometimes a cherry tree, as well as a rose or two — *Rosa gallica* is considered to be the original country garden rose. During the 17th and 18th centuries the range of plants expanded dramatically to include lots of today's favorites, as flowering plants from other countries were brought into Britain and found their way into cottage gardens via gardeners at the manor houses, as well as through friends and neighbors. New arrivals included jasmine, anemones, daylilies, fritillaries, hollyhocks, lychnis, lavender and clove pinks, clematis, auriculas, tulips and ranunculas, wallflowers and stocks, heliotrope, narcissus, and hyacinths. Shrub roses also made their appearance.

It was in the 19th century that what we consider the "typical" country garden really emerged. Now the gardens became more ordered into separate areas for flowers and produce, although some flowers continued to mingle happily with the fruit and vegetables. Topiary, practiced for centuries in formal gardens, became popular with rural gardeners eager to embellish their plots further and display their gardening skills, and a palette of favorite plants was established. As once rare plants became more common, they were ousted from grander gardens where style and status were all important, and eagerly collected by cottage gardeners who unwittingly took on the role of guardians. Without these keen early caregivers, many of our favorite plants might have vanished without a trace. It's just as satisfying today to grow plants handed down from family, friends, and neighbors in the

Lupines are indispensable in a country garden, flowering all summer long if you deadhead them after the first flush of bloom.

country garden tradition, and you may be preserving something very special for the future.

In the mid- to late 19th century hollyhocks, delphiniums, and lupines became increasingly common, soaring through foaming borders edged in lavenders and pinks, thrift and lady's mantle. For those that tended them, however, the gardens remained thoroughly functional as well as ornamental. At this point, country gardens suddenly achieved a new status, largely through the influence of the eminent gardener William Robinson (1838-1935). He hated formality and loved the simplicity of the jumble of plants, elevating cottage gardening into something of an art form. His contemporary Gertrude Jekyll (1843-1932) took this "art" of country gardening to new heights in her designs for abundant borders with carefully planned planting schemes for color, texture, and height.

Moving on

Carefully coordinated borders can be beautiful and satisfying, but country-style gardening is not about careful planning and restraint; it's more about letting things have their way. There's a great freedom in allowing nature to have a generous hand in your garden's design. A cottage garden is all about individuality; it is adamantly not about copying other people's taste and style. And since the essence is about following the spirit handed down by country gardeners through centuries rather than abiding by hard and fast rules, you can create just as attractive a garden in the town or the country, whether your house is old or new.

Meadowsweet and anthemis spill out from an informal corner bed in late summer.

This book provides guidelines to help you create and maintain a gorgeous and abundant garden, but it is not a rule book and every gardener's interpretation of this style will be different. The key is to keep the basics simple — including your choice of garden furniture and hard landscaping materials — and embellish the basics with plants. Then add more plants. Above all, never be nervous about trying something different, and enjoy the adventure that is country gardening.

FIRST STEPS

Working with the garden

The most attractive country gardens give the impression they have gently developed over generations. To recreate this feeling, it's best to take full account of the needs of the garden, as well as the needs of the gardener. This doesn't mean that you can't make your mark — after all, country gardens are anything but precious — but you'll find that it pays to be sensitive to what exists already.

The design of your garden will depend to some degree on what lies beyond it. You may want to organize your boundaries and screening to retain views and borrow shapes such as tall or majestic trees, interesting walls, or buildings. Other features will probably need to be hidden, and you will certainly want some privacy. You may also get useful clues to appropriate materials by noting what looks good locally.

Some gardeners will be starting from scratch with a brand-new plot, but most will be trying to transform an existing garden. It may be tempting to clear everything to start with a fresh canvas, but if you take on a garden in need of renovation, be patient. Try to live with it for several seasons before making radical changes. It is useful to see where the sunniest and windiest spots are through the year, where you need shade, or where you may need to let in more light by felling a tree, knocking down a structure, or moving a shed. Think hard before removing trees — do they provide necessary screens; is their shade useful or a hindrance; do they provide shelter; can old fruit trees be renovated or should they be replaced? True cottage gardeners use what already exists as a starting point and work from there.

Existing plants will give you good clues to the type of soil in your garden and its fertility, and anything that has been growing successfully for many years with little maintenance is likely to reward you generously if it is nurtured. You may find some unexpected treasures among the weeds, but even a weed-covered plot tells its own tale — stinging nettles indicate good fertility while a covering of docks and persistent annual weeds suggest the soil is in poor condition, and horsetail and mossy areas tell you where drainage is a problem.

Left: Plants in this border have been carefully selected for height, shape, and color to provide a cheerful and abundant impression as they spill over onto the irregular stone paved path.

Right: There's no restraint here where traditional country plants are spreading with abandon, tall happily mingling with short, self-seeders claiming any vacant space, and Rosa Paul's Himalayan Musk rambling up a tree.

GETTING STARTED

■ Make a list of what is in your garden already and note what is worth saving.

■ Are there interesting features nearby or is screening a priority?

■ Note which areas get the most sun and where shade is a bonus or a problem.

■ Take note of which existing plants thrive and the soil conditions they prefer.

■ Reuse as many plants and materials as you can.

■ Think carefully before removing any established trees; they may provide useful screens, windbreaks, shelter, or shade.

■ If you are in doubt about a variety of fruit tree, seek specialized advice; you may have an old local variety that is worth treasuring.

Considering all the elements

When you picture a country garden, the profusion and generosity of plants first spring to mind. You probably imagine heady scents and sensual shapes, with some vegetables, herbs, and fruit tucked among the flowers. But although plants do take center stage in a country garden, it shouldn't be just a plant repository, but rather a place for you and your family to use and enjoy. Gardens serve many purposes, and the trick is to find the right place for each one. Traditional country gardens grew and changed with the needs of the gardeners and what became available to them, so keep your ideas simple and functional from the start, allowing the garden to develop gradually from a basic framework.

Think about how your garden will be used and what you want from it. What are your needs? Do you want to cultivate most of the area; are you happy to maintain grass; how much time do you have to tend a garden? Are there certain times of year when you are particularly busy? Is it important to have a productive garden, or one that is predominantly ornamental? Will your garden be heavily used or not? Do you need privacy or do you want a more open garden? Be honest with yourself, because there's nothing more likely to deter you from gardening for life than taking on too much and watching everything slip into chaos.

There are a few universal elements that will suggest a basic framework: you will need some sort of boundary and entrance, and a path from gate to house. You will want to sit outside and enjoy your garden, so plan for at least one seating area and a place to eat outdoors in a sunny or partly shaded spot, preferably near the house. Include a "service area" for tool storage, a compost bin, and perhaps cold frames or a greenhouse — as well as garbage cans. You may also want a clothesline and perhaps an area for a children's climbing structure or play area. It may be a priority to create shade with trees or garden structures, or to erect screens for privacy, and of course you need as many spaces as possible for plants. Decide on what you need, then help your garden dictate the design.

Winter gardens can be inspiring — as well as havens for wildlife — when you leave plants standing and keep borders and boundaries clothed rather than clearing away the previous year's growth in the fall.

BASIC PRINCIPLES

- Keep referring to your garden when you are designing; walk around it at different times of day; experience which direction the wind comes from, how the sun falls; discover any particularly cool or damp areas.

- Avoid too many straight lines — add curves to long beds, steps, and paths, and vary the height of structures for an informal feel.

- Give plants the best chance by allocating them areas where they will flourish.

- Be as generous with your beds as possible — the larger the bed, the easier it will be to maintain and the more exuberant the planting will look.

- Leave as many spaces for plants as possible — even north-facing walls can support productive trees and attractive vines.

- Don't expect to plant heavily close to a hedge or underneath a large tree; both take a lot of nutrients from the soil.

Designing on paper

Once you have thought about what you want and need, measure your garden and draw a sketch of it on a large sheet of paper, clearly marking your boundaries, your house, and its entrances. Don't be daunted if you've never done this before; it's for your reference only, so it can be extremely scruffy or incredibly beautiful.

Mark trees and all permanent features that you intend to keep. Then cover the outline with a sheet of tracing paper and roughly mark all the places and spaces you want to include. Start with paths to the front and back doors — a fairly direct route is easiest. Walk around your garden while you're planning, to see how your ideas will work on the ground.

Choose a convenient spot for a sitting area — one facing south is best for a daytime sunspot, but a west-facing one will catch the most early evening sun. Perhaps include an arbor or tree for dappled shade over a sunny spot. Mark a utility area, with a path for easy access.

The rest of your garden will probably consist of flower and vegetable beds, fruit trees and bushes if you have room, and perhaps grassy areas or lawns. A pond is a valuable addition. Once you have marked the essentials, add arches and other decorative elements. Conventionally, country gardens are crammed with plants in every conceivable nook and cranny, and remember that the boundaries of your garden are valuable spaces for growing productive trees and shrubs, for supporting vines, and for sheltering slightly tender plants. In a small garden, use every space — a bench can provide a framework for climbing plants and could have tool storage underneath.

Note which areas of your garden are sunny, cool, shady, windswept, or sheltered. It will help you make sure you're placing features in the best possible positions. And your garden will be most successful if you give the plants the conditions they need.

Trees, hedges, and a subtle palette of plants create a very rustic feel in this courtyard garden where clipped box balls, containers, and small pieces of stone statuary provide a touch of formality.

Renovating a derelict garden

In one case, this initial sketch of a derelict cottage garden helped the owners decide to remove a mature ornamental tree that blocked late afternoon sunshine from the west-facing boundary and cast shade toward the back of the house. This opened up a new sunny area for flowers in a place that had formerly been suitable only for grass. Although the southwestern corner of the garden was cold under a tall hedge, the drawing reminded the owners that the hedge was necessary shelter from prevailing northeasterly winds, and hardy perennial vegetables such as rhubarb would thrive there.

As you can see below, simple but comprehensive notes help build up a valuable portrait of a garden and make easy work of replanning certain areas. Country gardens were never formally designed gardens, so they always work best if they start from a simple framework. This plot was conveniently divided into quarters, then subdivided with the most important features included. From this point it usually becomes fairly obvious where paths should go, and how beds should be laid out and divided. Add curves, and vary the width of paths and height of screens and plantings if you don't favor straight lines.

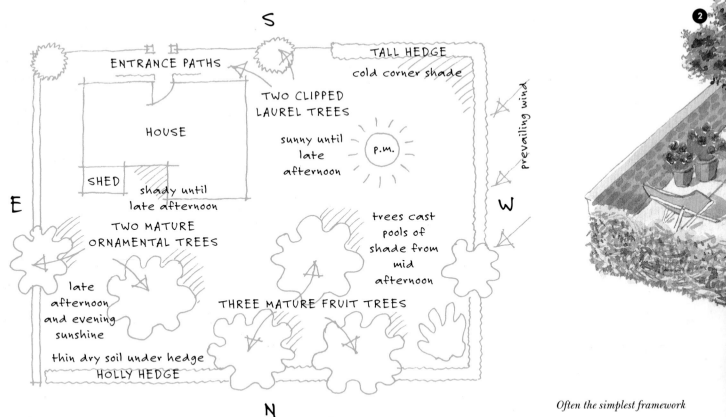

S

ENTRANCE PATHS

TALL HEDGE
cold corner shade

TWO CLIPPED
LAUREL TREES

HOUSE

sunny until
late
afternoon

P.M.

SHED
shady until
late afternoon

E

W

prevailing wind

TWO MATURE
ORNAMENTAL TREES

trees cast
pools of
shade from
mid
afternoon

late
afternoon
and evening
sunshine

THREE MATURE FRUIT TREES

thin dry soil under hedge
HOLLY HEDGE

N

Often the simplest framework works best. You can add further details and more plants as you live with the garden.

KEY

1 Shed
2 Plum tree
3 Flagstones with ground cover planting in between
4 Flower beds
5 Apple trees
6 Pear tree
7 Clipped laurel tree
8 Flower and herb bed
9 Vegetable bed
10 Damson tree
11 Mixed native hedge
12 Buddleia
13 Holly hedge

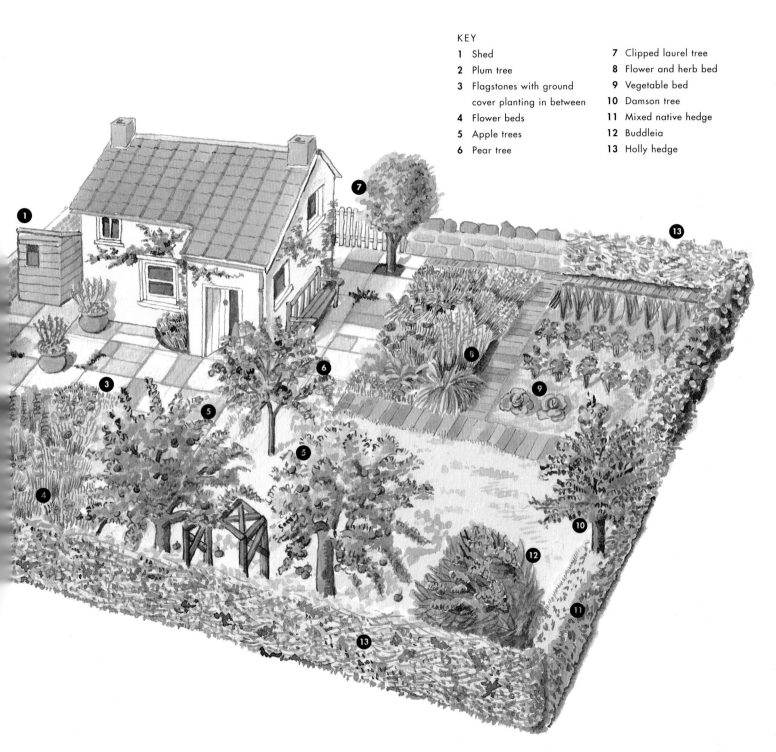

Noting sun and shade

Follow the course of the sun to make the most of the different areas of your garden, or add trees and screens for shade in very hot situations. Every garden will have sunny and shady areas, depending not only on its orientation and existing plantings, but also on neighboring features — even a sunny southwest-facing plot may be shadowed by tall buildings or mature trees nearby. You may need to erect fencing or hedging to deflect wind, and remember that west-facing boundaries make perfect places for even slightly tender plants. Even if you don't have enough spaces for vines, don't shy from erecting posts and wires or sections of trellis or woven fences to catch the sun; plants growing at different heights add to the feeling of plenty in a country garden.

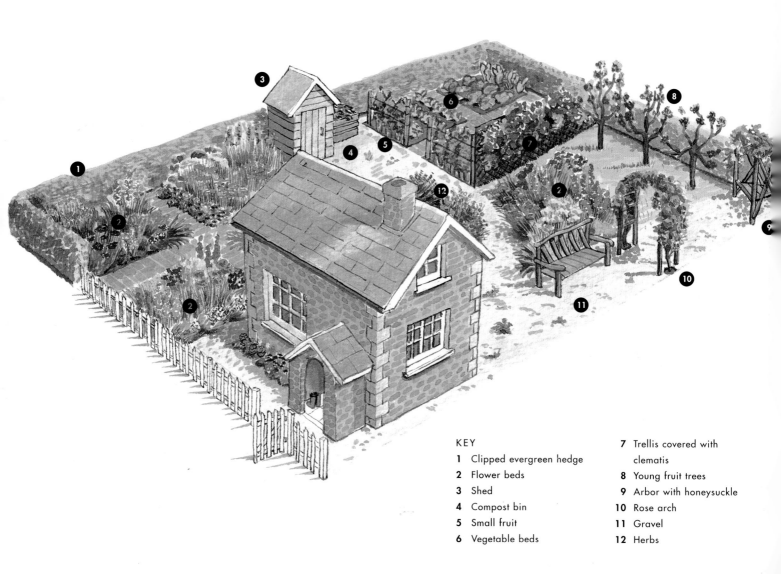

KEY

1 Clipped evergreen hedge
2 Flower beds
3 Shed
4 Compost bin
5 Small fruit
6 Vegetable beds
7 Trellis covered with clematis
8 Young fruit trees
9 Arbor with honeysuckle
10 Rose arch
11 Gravel
12 Herbs

Small traditional garden

Many gardens, particularly those attached to new houses, are broadly rectangular in shape. Keep the design very simple, then soften the lines with abundant planting and by varying the height and materials of your beds and boundaries. Unless you need space for children to play, try to avoid grass in a small country garden.

In this typical design for a very traditional small country garden, the seat is in a sunny spot right by the house looking over the flowers — a place to snatch a few moments at any time of day. Herbs are next to the house for easy picking, and a garden shed is also easily accessible, while the compost bins sit by the vegetables, where they will be most useful. A seat facing west catches the afternoon and early evening sun and would be lovely covered with scented roses and surrounded by fragrant plants. Let plants spill onto the paving, allow them to seed in your paths, or use containers to soften hard surfaces. In a restricted space, train fruit trees on a west-facing wall, underplanting with bulbs and herbs to make maximum use of the garden.

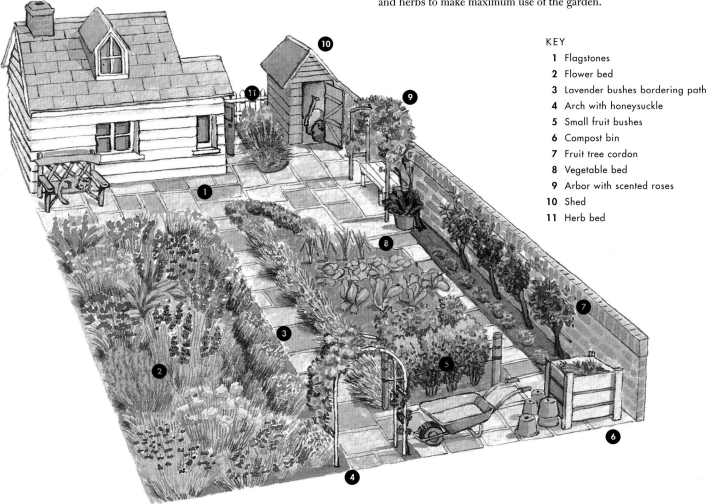

KEY

1 Flagstones
2 Flower bed
3 Lavender bushes bordering path
4 Arch with honeysuckle
5 Small fruit bushes
6 Compost bin
7 Fruit tree cordon
8 Vegetable bed
9 Arbor with scented roses
10 Shed
11 Herb bed

Larger rectangular garden

Whatever the size of your plot, stick to a simple division of the garden, and blur the lines with curves and plants. In a larger garden you may want to include a small orchard, or fill this space with flowers and train trees and climbers against the west-facing wall. Intersect large beds with paths. It's convenient to split a vegetable bed into four areas to rotate crops annually. A low lavender hedge would be a good border for a path beside fruit and vegetables. It looks good all season and also attracts helpful insects to keep bugs off your produce. Include a warm,

sheltered area for sitting out and entertaining, and add a tree or two to provide dappled shade if necessary. It's helpful to have a shed near a sitting area for convenient storage of outdoor furniture that is not in use. Place other tool storage and a compost bin beside your vegetable patch where you will need it most. Include a pond and somewhere to sit and enjoy watching the varied life it will attract, and surround the seat with fragrant flowers.

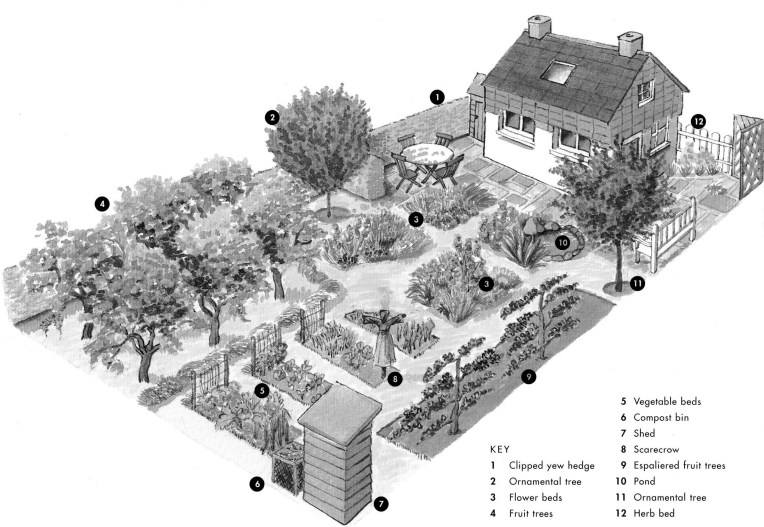

KEY

1 Clipped yew hedge	7 Shed
2 Ornamental tree	8 Scarecrow
3 Flower beds	9 Espaliered fruit trees
4 Fruit trees	10 Pond
5 Vegetable beds	11 Ornamental tree
6 Compost bin	12 Herb bed

Corner plot

The same principle of simple division of space applies to your garden whatever its shape. In this corner plot the garden is divided into a simple grid; variations can be made within the different segments. Beds and paths can be curved; paving materials varied with plants allowed to grow in the paths; arches and screens erected. Living screens of plant-covered trellis or fencing can be used to separate distinct areas. The vegetable plot could start life as a grassy lawn if you need somewhere for children to play; trees can be placed strategically within

or at the edge of flowerbeds to create pools of shade; boundaries can be planted and their heights varied.

Never be afraid to take up existing paving, change the route of paths, or make flowerbeds wherever you want them. The true essence of a country garden is abundant planting, but substantial areas of paving can be very versatile, providing a canvas for containers of all sorts, as well as the ideal spot for a garden table and chairs or a comfortable bench.

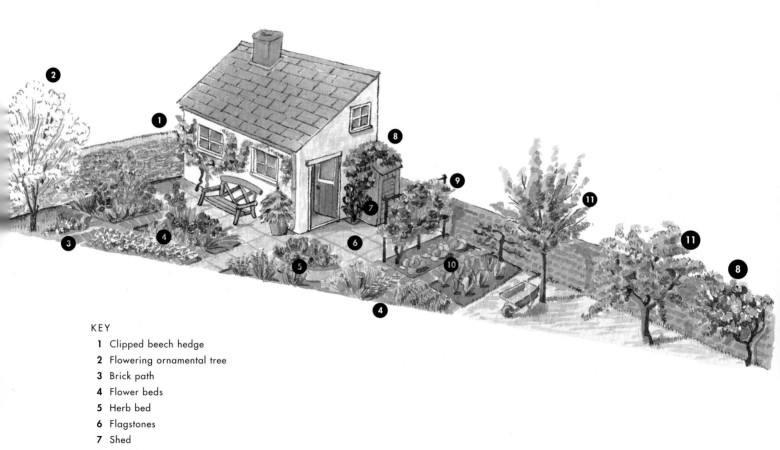

KEY
1 Clipped beech hedge
2 Flowering ornamental tree
3 Brick path
4 Flower beds
5 Herb bed
6 Flagstones
7 Shed
8 Climbing rose
9 Floral screen
10 Vegetable beds
11 Fruit trees

Planning boundaries

A priority for the first country gardeners was fencing the garden from the adjacent field, to keep marauding animals out and domestic ones in. Today a fence or hedge is more likely to be needed for privacy, shelter, or security — or all three. But boundaries don't have to be barriers. In some situations you may want to keep your garden fairly open to take advantage of a view or a particular feature. As a general rule, don't let your boundaries shut you off unless it is really necessary. Remember that the need for privacy is much greater in summer than winter, and you may be able to create private areas with screening and plantings within the garden. Some annual climbers are fast growers and combined with trellises, are ideal for a quick summer screen.

Your choice of boundary material depends on space, situation, and sometimes on what is typical locally — try to help your garden fit into the surrounding landscape. If you want to retain a slightly open feeling, a fence constructed of vertical wood palings is traditional, and picket fences are attractive. Panels of wooden trellis are widely available and make very cheap and versatile fences that can be planted with a variety of productive and ornamental climbing plants. Cut

Oriental poppies have been popular for centuries in country gardens; here their bright and voluptuous splashes of color brighten the entrance to a utilitarian poultry enclosure.

lumber fencing panels are easy to buy and install, but if your garden is buffeted by wind, limit your use of solid panels because a solid barrier will trap wind and create problems. If you can find them, panels of woven willow wattle make attractive and useful informal fences, ideal for growing plants through.

Hedges are relatively cheap to establish; they form a wonderful backdrop to any country garden and are particularly good in windy

Tall purple campanulas compete with giant spires of foxtail lilies in this flowerbed to create brilliant sparks of color against the somber stone wall in the background.

situations because they allow some wind to filter through. A boundary of mixed native hedging plants makes an attractive border to any country-style garden, but it suits a rural situation best, while a neatly clipped evergreen hedge is equally at home in a heavily built-up environment.

If there are lots of stone or brick walls in your area, consider constructing a wall to border at least one edge of your garden. Whatever you choose, try to keep a feeling of informality, even where you have long lines and sharp corners; smudge the edges through varying heights and mixing materials of fences, walls, or hedges, and through plantings.

Making an entrance

Once the boundary is erected, you may need a gate, and a path from gate to doorway. The first thing any visitor to your garden will see is the gate — although it may seem to be an insignificant part of your whole garden, it is worth taking trouble over the design. Think about the impression you want to give, and think about the local landscape and whether you want to cut yourself off from it or maintain a link. A rustic gate, for example, can be suitable in even urban areas to contrast your style of garden with the harsher environment, but a modern urban-style gate will always look out of place in the country. You should also choose your gate according to the boundary fence or hedge it pierces. In general, a low gate suits a high wall or hedge, while a high or solid gate or door can look appropriate set in an informal boundary hedge of trees and tall shrubs.

The height of your boundary and the distance of your gateway from the house will help to dictate the sort of entrance you choose. If your gate is near your front door, you will probably want to keep it low so it does not block any light, but if it is some distance away, you could think about placing an arch over it. Few gardeners have ever been able to resist dressing up the basics, so you can follow their example and clothe a welcoming entrance arch with different combinations of vines, from the obvious choice of sweetly scented roses and honeysuckle, to scarlet runner beans, in the true country-garden tradition of combining simplicity with ingenuity.

A low wooden gate is traditional and looks equally at home between two sections of hedge, fence, or wall. Old-fashioned low wrought-iron gates can be beautiful and romantic, particularly when set into a wall with an arch over the gate, making visitors feel they are embarking on a journey into a secret garden. But ornate modern wrought-iron gates look out of place, and double gates really are too grand for a simple country garden entrance.

From gateway to doorway

Traditionally the path from gate to cottage door was straight, the most direct route, but you don't need to be restrained by convention, just function. There's something satisfyingly logical about a straight path, and there's no need to be afraid it might be too formal or rigid for an informal garden; plants will soon enough spill over the edges to soften the lines. On a long stretch you can also add an informal feel by varying the width of the path along its length, and even the straightest path doesn't need to have parallel sides. Varying the width is a particularly good ruse to employ in a small garden, because it can make the space seem larger.

When planning any path, consider first where it has to go, then what it is to be used for — how much traffic will it take. You will need to be able to easily access your front and back doors, and also get to sitting areas, the utility area that houses your compost bin, and your tool storage. Any path should be at least wide enough to take a wheelbarrow. It's best to make paths as generous as possible; plants will soon colonize them and disguise the width.

An arch is a brilliant addition to a straight path. It will not only frame and enclose the path, adding height and solidity, but can also add an element of surprise. Even the most basic structure can turn a journey along a straight path into something of an adventure, particularly when it is covered with a variety of climbing plants.

A straight brick path leading to the front door is softened by billowing clouds of informal flowers, with two standard roses adding an upright touch by the door.

GATES AND PATHS

■ A simple low wooden gate is traditional, appropriate, and attractive.

■ Add height and interest by framing a path or gate with an arch.

■ Scented roses and honeysuckle are traditional companions for an entrance arch, but climbing vegetables and annuals provide a new take on style.

■ Think about the uses of your garden and where a path should lead.

■ Don't be afraid of straight paths; plants soon spill over and soften the edges.

■ Varying the width of a path helps add interest to a small garden.

Lady's mantle is a traditional country garden edging plant; here it has spread to change the shape of a once straight gravel path. Its acid yellow flowers provide a perfect foil for pink and lavender blossoms.

31

Planning beds

Abundant flower displays are the hallmark of a country garden, so be generous with planting spaces. The most appealing country gardens look as though the plants have just sprung up of their own accord and colonized the ground over decades, but you can get this feeling in a season or two if you start with a good basic structure while leaving room for improvisation. There are really no rules except to plant generously and let the plants talk — you must match plants to the right conditions, so don't expect a drought-loving candidate to sit happily next to something that likes moist, water-retentive soil.

Other people's gardens, books, and television programs can provide brilliant inspiration, but don't get too seduced by them, or by mouth-watering descriptions in plant catalogs. First decide what is most important to you. How much time do you have to spend working in your garden? Is low maintenance a priority? Do you want your garden to provide year-round interest or are you happy for it to slumber quietly through the winter? Do you want to be traditional or to mix old with new? Are you interested in conserving old varieties? Is it important for the garden to attract wildlife? Do you want to mix herbs and vegetables with your flowers?

Find out as much as possible about the plants you want to grow, particularly their height and spread, their preferred conditions, and their flowering time. Foliage can provide as much interest as flowers — think of the acid green, dew-catching flutes of emerging lady's mantle *(Alchemilla mollis)* in spring, hairy poppy leaves, silver-gray pinks, and brilliantly colored chard leaves as well as evergreens and grasses.

Keep the height of plants in scale with your garden and your beds: while a few large plants can be used to make a small space seem larger, you ideally want a good mixture of heights and shapes for an informal feel. Take particular account of plants' flowering seasons to plan for continuously attractive beds — Oriental poppies *(Papaver orientale)*, for example, are a must for early summer, but they collapse

These generous beds show how the colors and shapes of foliage can be as important as the blossoms; the clipped box balls on the left provide winter structure when perennials have died back.

to leave a mass of browning foliage and need something to take the space in front of them in mid-summer. Allow generous planting spaces — plants grow best if they are given enough room, and it's easy to fill gaps with annuals while beds are filling out. Note whether tall plants are self-supporting or need help — foxgloves and aconites don't, delphiniums do — and try to provide supportive neighbors where necessary.

The essence of a country garden is a bit of disorder and a degree of anarchy among the plants, so don't be too rigid about heights and shapes and tasteful color combinations. A standard way of planning a long bed is to draw it on graph paper, divide it into blocks graduating in size from back to front and center to edge, and fill them in, but this is much too rigid for a traditional country garden. Of course it's sensible to keep height at the back of a long bed, or in the center of a large bed, and graduate to low-growing candidates at the front, but you should also allow for some tall subjects to shoot up above lower ones throughout beds, seemingly at random in typical country-garden style. Having said that, it's nonetheless best to start with a fairly strong initial framework by planting groups of plants matched by species, color, shape, or texture, then fill in the spaces. Mix grasses with herbaceous plants, let annuals romp beneath and through shrubs, and don't forget bulbs. It always looks good to edge beds alongside paths and paving with lax plants that escape from the beds so you can scarcely tell where soil ends and hard surface begins.

Traditionally, country gardens were at their most exuberant in summer, but we have such a great choice of plants today that you can kickstart your display in early spring with vibrant bulbs and keep going right into deepest fall and winter with whispering ornamental grasses and perennials with interesting seedheads as well as winter bloomers, where winters are not too severe, and evergreen subjects for year-round structure. Although some plants — including sweetly scented pinks and sweet Williams, tall spires of delphiniums, foxgloves, and hollyhocks, blowsy heads of poppies, and delicate love-in-a-mist — have come to symbolize country-garden planting, don't ever feel restricted by convention. Early cottage gardeners used whatever plants they could get — wild plants, snippets gleaned from gardeners at large houses, and seeds and cuttings from friends and neighbors. And if they came across anything new, they snapped it up. So feel free.

USING PLANTS

■ Match plants with places — make sure the conditions suit the plants.

■ Neighboring plants should have matching strengths — don't plant something very vigorous next to a reluctant grower, or the first will crowd out the other.

■ Plant generously — large groups of plants simplify planning and form pleasing patterns. Fill gaps between developing shrubs and perennials with annuals.

■ Take note of the habits of plants and mix clump-forming plants with those that spread in loose informal drifts.

■ Use obelisks and other supports for vines among your herbaceous plants.

■ Plan for as long a flowering period as possible — extend it with spring bulbs, summer annuals, fall foliage, and grasses.

■ Walls and hedges can provide shelter for slightly tender plants as well as spaces for vines.

■ Leave room for surprises — if a plant springs up where it really doesn't look good, it's easy enough to transplant it, but you just might stumble across a winning combination.

Don't be afraid to mix colors shamelessly. These magenta lupines look quite at home peeking through yellow roses alongside other mauve, pink, and red shades.

Planning vegetable beds

When planning for vegetables, first take account of what you and your family like to eat. Rows of cabbages, Brussels sprouts, and kale look traditional and attractive, but there's no point growing them just for show. Country gardens habitually include a dedicated vegetable plot, which should be decorative as well as functional. Many vegetables thrive when planted among flowers that attract beneficial insects to keep pests down, and marigolds and flowering herbs should always be included. Cheerful poppies, generous sunflowers, and scrambling nasturtiums are excellent companions to rows of vegetables, and a wigwam of climbing beans looks at home in a flower bed and decorative in a vegetable bed if you mix climbing flowers such as morning glories with the beans.

Most vegetables need rich soil and a sunny position, so don't relegate a vegetable bed to a shady area. Keep the soil well fed with manure and compost, and avoid planting the same crop in the same place two years running in order to keep soil healthy. Traditionally, potatoes and tomatoes, legumes, brassicas, and most root vegetables are planted in rotation on a four-year cycle (see below), but you don't need to follow this routine slavishly.

Consider sowing and harvesting times. Salad leaves such as lettuces grow very quickly and can present you with a glut. Successional sowing — sowing a row of seed every two weeks or so — staggers your harvest. In cool areas, try the same technique for radishes and spinach.

To keep soil in the best condition, avoid walking on it any more than necessary, so try to have adjacent areas of your plot clear at the same time. Straight rows of vegetables are easy to sow and hoe, but planting in blocks looks less formal and is also easy to manage. The main problem with vegetable beds is keeping them weed free, so sow into warm, well-cleared soil to give your crops the best start, and interplant slow-growing plants, like alliums or brassicas, with faster-growing salads to allow the minimum amount of bare soil.

In areas that will be left uncultivated for any length of time, consider growing a green manure to keep the ground covered and stop weeds from moving in. (See page 47 for more information.)

CROP ROTATION

Try to plant vegetables in a four-year rotation cycle. Plant legumes in one row or bed; brassicas in another; root vegetables in a third; potatoes and tomatoes in a fourth. Leafy greens can be planted with brassicas or potatoes. Onions are usually planted with legumes, but leeks more often with members of the potato family. Salads can be fitted in anywhere there is space, or allot them room with legumes. Celery, corn, and squash thrive alongside potatoes. In the second year, move the legumes group from row A to row B, in the third year from row B to row C, and so on.

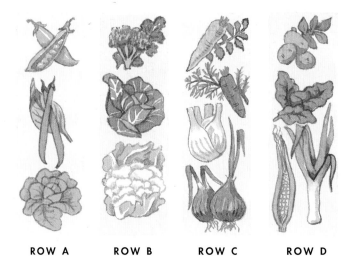

ROW A   **ROW B**   **ROW C**   **ROW D**

KEY

ROW A: Legumes (peas, beans) and salads, and any fast maturing vegetables.

ROW B: Brassicas (cabbages, cauliflowers, broccoli, sprouts, kales) and any perennial vegetables.

ROW C: Root vegetables (parsnips, carrots, fennel) and onions. Salads can be grown between them.

ROW D: Potatoes, spinach, corn, leeks. Tomatoes should also be planted in this group.

Fava beans are supported by stakes, while colorful chives mingle with salad vegetables and tubs of marigolds edge the path in this small kitchen garden.

PLANNING ROTATIONS

■ Different crops take different nutrients from the soil. If you change crops each year, you replenish the soil with different elements and prevent crop-specific pests and diseases from building up in the soil.

■ Bear in mind that potatoes and squash are greedy feeders.

■ Legumes (peas and beans) add nitrogen to the soil.

■ Leafy greens and brassicas thrive in nitrogen-rich soil.

■ Onions like rich soil.

■ Carrots and parsnips will "fork" (or split) in soil that is too rich.

■ Salads and fast-growing vegetables are happy in any well-fed soil.

Planning herbs

Early country gardeners considered herbs more important as medicines than as flavorings, so plan to include some herbs especially for their healing properties as well as your favorites for culinary use.

Some herbs are decorative and fragrant flowering plants, and are also good for the general health of your garden because they attract bees, butterflies, and other helpful insects. A bed of lavender or hyssop in a vegetable garden brings lacewings and other insect predators into the garden to help keep bugs off their neighbors.

Many herbs thrive in light, sandy soil in a sunny spot, although they are very adaptable and most will sit happily in a richer soil, as long as it is not cold and waterlogged — they hate damp feet. Thyme, marjoram, winter and summer savory, chamomile, borage, hyssop, and other herbs from dry southern climates will grow in gravel or cracks in paving and spread freely. Parsley has a deep root and thrives in vegetable beds, as do statuesque herbs such as lovage and angelica. Because these can reach about 10 feet (3 m) they are also suitable for wide beds. Fennel, dill, rosemary, and sage are invaluable for the kitchen and the easiest of garden plants, but rampant tansy and mints should always be contained — either planted in pots or in submerged boxes or a trough to confine their spread. Tender basil is a must for summer cooking, but young plants seem to act as slug magnets, so many people have most success growing them in pots, where they can keep an eye on them.

You can dot herbs around the garden, or copy a traditional herb garden design such as a circle with divisions between the beds like the spokes of a wheel. An old sink full of herbs near the kitchen door is practical and attractive. Knot gardens might be considered rather upscale for a country garden but within any formal layout, a planting can be informal, mixing heights, textures, and colors.

Plan a knot design carefully on graph paper first, and then transfer your design to the soil using sand trickled from a bottle to mark out the beds before planting low, outlining hedges of box, lavender, or santolina, or even chives or parsley. Fill the spaces with perennial or annual herbs, or mix them with perennial plants, including bulbs for late winter and spring showing.

This rather formal herb garden borrows heavily from the country garden tradition of mixing herbs, vegetables, and flowers in the same area.

HINTS ON HERBS

■ Most kitchen herbs need sun and light soil. Prepare the soil well, adding grit and sand along with compost if it is at all heavy.

■ Rosemary and lavender make good hedges in warm areas, or can be clipped into balls for points of interest.

■ Plant herbs for the kitchen near the door. If there's no suitable spot, grow them in containers.

■ Herbs with small leaves are usually sun-loving; those with larger fleshier leaves often tolerate shade and damper conditions.

■ Gray-leaved herbs always prefer light soil and sun.

■ Meadowsweet, angelica, bergamot, marsh mallow, and valerian will grow in a damp, shady bed.

Planning small fruit

A traditional place for raspberries and gooseberries is at one end of a vegetable plot or orchard. Both gooseberries and currant bushes often formed a boundary hedge in European country gardens, along with the ubiquitous blackberry, acting as effective barriers as well as bearing fruit. In a small garden, a hedge may still be the best location for them.

You don't have to forsake small fruit if your space is very limited. You can, for example, grow summer-fruiting raspberries trained in a column, and fall-fruiting varieties make fine freestanding bushes that can be cut down to the ground after fruiting. Some gooseberries can be grown as standards on stems about 4 feet (1.5 m) tall, which also allows you to underplant them with low-growing shrubs and bulbs.

Wild blackberries may have a better flavor than cultivated versions, but their rampant habit doesn't endear them to most gardeners, so there are less aggressive cultivars to choose from. The best way to grow them is trained along wires against a fence or wall. Include them if you can — they make wonderful wildlife havens, providing food and shelter late in the year. If you can't contemplate blackberries, substitute loganberries or tayberries, which are crosses between raspberries and blackberries, and crop heavily if they are planted in well-manured soil.

All berries fruit best in sun, but will still crop in shade, and rhubarb — sometimes classified as a vegetable — flourishes in a cool, damp, and shady situation. No country garden should be without strawberries; if you have space, grow them in their own bed. They are also very decorative with their attractive flowers and fruits, and the small-fruited varieties make particularly good edging plants for beds and paths, fruiting happily under the foliage of other plants.

Grapes were grown in northern Europe as well as in sunnier climates from medieval times, and many early country gardens featured a grapevine. You must choose cultivars carefully to get fruit in colder areas, but grapevines are worth considering if only for their attractive foliage and fall color. If you keep them cut back hard to limit their growth, you may get a reasonable crop of grapes as a bonus.

You can successfully grow figs and vines over a framework to create a succulent and productive shady space in a sunny garden.

PLANTING AND TRAINING SUMMER-FRUITING RASPBERRIES ON POST AND WIRE

1 Prepare an area at least 3 feet (90 cm) wide, and manure the ground well. Construct permanent supports from stout posts 10 feet (3 m) apart supporting three lengths of wire at heights of 30 inches (75 cm), 42 inches (1.1 m) and 5 feet (1.5 m). Plant canes 15-18 inches (35-45 cm) apart in well-manured ground. Cut these back to a bud about 10 inches (25 cm) above the ground.

2 During the summer, as the plants throw out new canes, tie these in to the support wires. When they are established, cut out the old canes that were shortened at planting time.

3 As soon as they have cropped, cut back all fruited canes to ground level and tie the new growth to the support wires.

4 When new canes reach 6 inches (15 cm) above the topmost wire they should be cut off (tipped). In spring, before the growing season begins, tip prune all canes to a healthy bud. As canes lengthen, loop new growth through the wires and tie it in.

Raspberries can be trained for their first year along twine, to be replaced with permanent wires after fruiting.

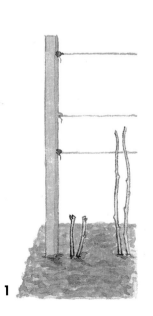

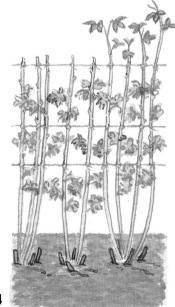

1   **2**   **3**   **4**

Planning tree fruit

All country gardens should include a productive fruit tree or two. Today the wide choice of rootstocks makes it possible to include apples, plums, and peaches in quite small gardens. As well, fruit trees can be pruned into space-saving and appealing shapes, flat against walls or fences, or into fruiting arches. Damsons, crabapples, and bush cherries or plums can be included in a hedge. Purchase trees on semi-dwarfing rootstock for smaller gardens. Steer clear of some of the most compact shapes, such as those that fruit close to a pole-like stem, or miniatures marketed "for patios" or "for containers," which are too contrived for a country garden.

Your choice will largely depend on the space available and what grows best in your area, but try to include an apple, pear, and plum if possible. Be careful when siting fruit trees because they will be in position for several decades at least. Think about the eventual size of the tree, and don't plant a large tree too close to a boundary. Ideally, they should be protected from strong cold winds, and placed where they won't overshadow the rest of the garden but will provide dappled cover in summer — to sit under and to allow shade-loving plants to flourish.

If you have room for only one fruit tree, make it an apple, and choose a self-pollinating variety if there are no other fruit trees nearby. Quinces, crabapples, and mulberries are beautiful and productive trees but require space; peaches and figs probably found their way into European country gardens several hundred years ago and are excellent candidates to grow against warm walls. Choose varieties carefully. With fruit trees it is generally best to stick to traditional varieties and tried-and-tested country-garden subjects. Find out about any local varieties

and, if possible, plant these. They will grow well in your area, and you may also be helping to preserve old favorites. If you have space for several trees, plan so they will blossom and fruit at different times to extend the pleasure of spring blossom and fall harvest.

Right: Fruit trees grow very happily trained flat against walls or fences, and tender fruit likes to be grown against a warm south or west-facing wall. Morello cherries will flourish against a north-facing wall.

Below: For maximum productivity in a small garden, train fruit trees as cordons against a wall as this technique encourages the heaviest fruiting.

Fan training is ideal for slightly tender fruit such as peaches and figs.

Espalier training is most popular for apples and pears.

Cordons should be grown at an angle against fences and walls, or trained from straight stems to form fruiting arches.

Soil

Whatever plans you have for your garden, they will succeed if you get your soil in good condition. It's horribly tempting to rush out and buy the plants of your choice to grow immediately, but don't succumb. There is no substitute for good preparation.

Plants need to get their food, water, and air from the soil, so it must be in the best possible condition to support them. The ideal soil is crumbly enough to have plenty of spaces for air and water within it, and spongy enough to hold onto the moisture and air. It should be rich in minerals and contain masses of organic matter that burrowing insects and microorganisms can convert into plant food.

Depending on where you live and how well your garden has been tended, your soil will be acid, alkaline, or neutral. This is determined by the amount of calcium or lime it contains. Some plants such as heathers, camellias, and rhododendrons need acid soil, while many herbs and aromatic plants need an alkaline environment, but most plants grow happily in soils that are neutral or slightly acid or alkaline.

Soil types

The good news is that whatever soil you start with, you can transform it into a fertile growing environment, although some soils present more of a challenge than others. Sandy soils have large soil particles, which means they don't stick together very well; they are very crumbly and easy to work, but hard to keep in good condition because they drain fast. They need the addition of copious quantities of organic matter to add nutrition and substance. Clay soils are made up of tiny mineral particles that stick together like glue. They tend to be solid and heavy to work, and difficult for air and water to penetrate, so they can get stale or waterlogged. Lighten clay by digging in grit as well as masses of organic matter. Loam soils contain a mixture of small and large soil particles. They are crumbly, full of nutrients, and easy to work, but still need to be fed with organic matter to keep them in tip-top condition. Peat soils tend to be crumbly and rich in organic matter, but are always acid and often wet — they may need to be drained and should be fed with lots of compost.

A QUESTION OF pH

The balance of minerals in most soils can be improved through regular cultivation and addition of organic matter. If you have any doubts about the fertility of your soil, test its pH every two or three years. The pH indicates how acid or alkaline it is. In very acid or alkaline soils, plant roots have difficulty in extracting whatever minerals may be available to them. These soils may also harm or deter the soil organisms that help keep your soil healthy.

Gladioli, sweet scented phlox, alliums, and lavender are happy companions in this moderately light soil, but complain if they get waterlogged.

Compost

Once all waste had to be recycled because there was nothing else to do with it. If country gardeners kept pigs or chickens, scraps of vegetable and garden waste were fed to the animals, and their manure was put into a heap, left to rot, and then spread on the garden to feed the plants. If there were no domestic barnyard animals, anything that would rot was put in a pile and later distributed over the garden. Composting is a commonsense part of country gardening, turning your garbage into valuable natural fertilizer — for free.

Compost contains all the major elements that plants need for optimum growth, as well as necessary trace elements. It feeds your soil and also helps build it into the ideal condition to accept nutrients. Compost makes sandy soils heavier and spongier, and it makes clay soils less sticky and lighter, helping the soils to accept and use nutrients effectively. It makes peat soils less acid and chalk soils less alkaline. It is a living substance, made up of microorganisms and the organic matter they are constantly helping to decompose, so it works with your soil to release nutrients when plants need them most, slowly in cool spring and fall weather when soil organisms are sluggish and plant growth slow, and faster as soil temperatures heat up and plants are in stages of rapid growth.

Composting is an entirely natural process, and any garbage left on the soil will eventually rot and be taken back into the soil. But few gardeners want to leave debris lying around, so make space for a compost pile, or at least a bin, and throw onto it vegetable and garden waste, plus an occasional sprinkling of manure and a bit of water in very dry times. Choose a method of composting to suit you: a wooden bin or pile is traditional, but needs good supplies of waste and takes at least six months to produce useable compost; plastic tumbling bins can produce compost in around six weeks, and worm bins are ideal for kitchen scraps, regularly producing small quantities of highly concentrated liquid fertilizer. If you have large supplies of fallen leaves, compost them separately in a wire mesh cage to create a rich soil improver.

Compost ingredients

You can make an art of composting, sorting different ingredients before you add them and building piles of neat layers of alternating materials, but all a successful compost pile needs is regular supplies of varied material, circulation of air, enough moisture to keep it slightly damp, and a sheltered site.

Mix a variety of materials that are fast and slower to compost, and let nature do the rest. The only rules are never to add more than a $2^1/2$ inch (6 cm) layer of grass clippings at one time because they can stifle air circulation, and try to mix them with fibrous material. Add regular supplies of fruit and vegetable scraps, eggshells, teabags and

The best compost contains a good variety of different plant material. Vegetable waste and annual weeds are ideal staple ingredients.

coffee waste, soft prunings and young clippings, shredded leaves, pet bedding — but not cat or dog feces — old plants, and cut flowers. Every so often, add a layer of quick-rotting material such as poultry manure, comfrey leaves, young weeds, nettles, horsetail, manure, and grass cuttings. Urine also speeds up the composting processes. Materials that are fairly slow to rot, such as egg cartons and cardboard tubes, wood ash, woody prunings, corncobs, sawdust, and old woolen clothing, should be added in moderation. Cover your compost with a lid or a piece of old carpet to keep in the heat that is generated as the materials rot. Some people like to turn their pile every few weeks in summer to aerate it, but this is largely a matter of preference.

GROWING COMPOST AND GREEN MANURE

Green manure is a crop grown specifically to be chopped down and returned to the soil. It is a way of covering bare ground, preventing soil erosion or weed infestation, while adding fertility. In a large garden, or if you need something to fill space for a while, it may also be worth growing some plants specifically for the compost pile.

■ Legumes, members of the bean family, are good green manure because they collect nitrogen, which is needed for healthy leaf growth, in their roots and return high levels of it to the soil.

■ Perennial clovers and vetch are hardy legumes, excellent for covering soil all winter; till them into the soil in spring.

■ *Phacelia tanacetifolia* produces an excellent, nutritious summer green manure.

■ Red or yellow clover adds nitrogen to a depleted soil.

■ Grow comfrey especially for the compost pile; it provides many elements and speeds up the composting process.

■ Sunflowers are worth growing for the compost pile — they are bulky, nutrient-rich, and high in fiber, especially useful when you need to incorporate quantities of nitrogen-rich grass clippings.

It's well worth growing comfrey for the compost heap, where it helps other ingredients break down quickly and efficiently.

Digging

The prime purpose of digging is to incorporate compost and manure along with the air that plant roots and soil organisms need. Digging loosens soils by breaking up heavy clods to allow roots easier penetration and providing channels for water to soak into the ground. This is particularly important in a garden that has been neglected, and in gardens on new building developments where the soil is often poor-quality topsoil dumped over a hard crust.

Dig heavy clay soil only in dry conditions. If you try to work wet clay, it becomes even more solid and sticky. The best time to dig it is in fall, incorporating lots of well-rotted manure and compost or leaf mold, and perhaps some sand, and leaving winter frosts to help break up clods into smaller crumbs. You must always add organic matter when you dig it or it will become less, rather than more, nutrient-retentive. Never leave a sandy soil bare over winter, but cover bare spaces in your vegetable plot with a thick mulching layer of organic matter or, better still, a growing crop of green manure.

Tilling can take the pain out of digging a large plot, but add plenty of organic matter as you turn the soil, and be aware that the ground may still need careful weeding since you might have chopped up pieces of perennial weed roots and spread them around as you tilled.

If your garden contains plants that you want to keep, just dig around them, feeding the surrounding soil as you dig. If they are in the wrong place, prepare the ground in the area where you want to move them, water the ground well, lift them, and transfer them, watering well when you replant and adding compost in the planting hole. As long as you don't let them suffer stress by drying out or damaging their roots, most plants transplant very easily.

Try not to step on freshly dug soil or you can damage its structure; the less you walk on your soil, the healthier it will stay.

DOUBLE-DIGGING

Neglected soils benefit from double-digging, where both the subsoil and topsoil are thoroughly loosened and organic is matter added. It is hard work, but excellent for clearing the ground and adding fertility. You should only ever need to do it once!

1 Divide the area to be dug lengthwise into strips about 18 inches (45 cm) wide and remove the topsoil to one spade's depth (**A**) along the nearside. Barrow the soil to the other edge of the bed and leave it there.

2 Loosen the soil in the base of the trench with the tines of your garden fork and shovel on a generous amount of farmyard manure or garden compost. Then remove a strip of topsoil alongside it (**B**) in the same way as before, this time turning the resulting soil into your first trench, removing weeds and mixing the soil with the manure as you go.

3 Loosen the soil in the base of the resulting trench as before, add manure or compost, then repeat the procedure with a third strip of topsoil (**C**).

4 Repeat the procedure across the bed until you have turned the furthest strip (**D**) into the trench to its left.

5 Fill the final trench with the topsoil that you removed from the first strip (**A**).

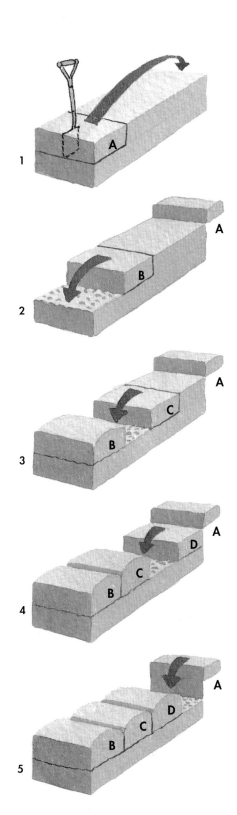

HOW TO DIG

■ Dig clay soil only in dry weather, adding plenty of organic matter.

■ Only add very well-rotted compost, leaf mold, or manure to clay soil; never add straw or fresh manure. These materials do not decompose quickly and will make the soil more impenetrable and stale.

■ Dig sandy soil in the spring, before planting; never leave it bare.

■ Sandy soil benefits from well-rotted manure or compost, which improve water retention and add nutrients.

■ If you double-dig your soil well before you plant, you should never need to dig it again. Just keep feeding it with compost and organic fertilizers.

■ It can be easier to dig clay using a fork rather than a spade. A fork aerates the soil and doesn't compact it.

Weed control

Thorough cultivation, digging, and weeding by hand are the best ways to clear ground, but be realistic. If you inherit a patch full of persistent perennial weeds such as quack grass and thistles, perhaps with dandelions, creeping buttercups, and docks for good measure, decide whether you need to tackle it all at once. If you attack perennial weeds halfheartedly, they will keep returning, robbing your soil of nutrients that other plants need, choking roots, and generally causing you a headache. So if time is limited, concentrate on thoroughly clearing one section of your garden at a time. Dig weedy areas with a fork, not a spade, which can cut through pieces of root and leave tiny segments in the ground to become new problems.

To curb an annual weed problem, weed your garden well by hand in early spring, then hoe regularly on dry days throughout spring and summer. Never hoe on damp days; it can encourage weeds to spread more. You'll never get rid of annual weeds entirely because seeds come in on the wind and with wildlife and live in your soil for many years.

However, as you add compost and manure to your soil, the weed problem will lessen, because most weeds are opportunists, designed to colonize waste places and therefore less fertile soil. If you have a persistent annual weed problem, be sure to hoe or cut them down in summer before they seed.

It is a good idea to warm the ground where you intend to plant vegetables by covering it with plastic or row cover material two or three weeks before you sow your first vegetable seeds. This tricks weeds into early germination; then you can hoe them off and avoid competition with your vegetables when they are most vulnerable. Keep as much of your soil covered as possible at all times; for example, plant quick-growing salads in between longer-maturing vegetables, and annuals among perennials, to give weeds less space to make their homes, or use mulches. These can be used to smother perennial weeds and to prevent annual weeds from germinating, while improving soil texture and fertility and conserving moisture.

Left: Cover beds with a light mulch but keep it clear of onion bulbs, which need to be baked in the sun. Marigolds are good kitchen garden companions as their root excretions and scent can help deter weeds and pests.

Right: The closer you plant your rows of vegetables, the less space for weeds to colonize; you should need to hoe between the plants only once or twice as they grow.

WEED-EXCLUDING MULCHES

COMPOST AND WELL-ROTTED MANURE
Nourishes soil and plants. Use on vegetables and flowerbeds.

AUTUMN LEAVES
Well-rotted leaf mold is an excellent antiweed and conditioning mulch.

STRAW
Partially rotted straw is a useful mulch on perennial beds.

GRASS MOWINGS
Thin (2 in./5 cm) layers of rotted grass clippings add nutrients, conserve moisture, and suppress weeds.

WOOD SHAVINGS/SHREDDED BARK
Attractive weed suppressor, but they rob the soil of nitrogen, so don't incorporate them into the soil.

BLACK PLASTIC SHEET
Ideal for clearing badly infested land. Leave in place for one year, then cultivate the land well, adding lots of organic matter before planting.

WOVEN PLASTIC/POLYPROPYLENE SHEET
Excellent weed-suppressing mulch for permanent plantings.

FLATTENED CARDBOARD BOXES
Alternative to plastic for smothering perennial weeds.

Natural pest control

Slugs, snails, aphids, mites, thrips, caterpillars, and soil grubs appear in every garden, but they need not cause serious problems. Traditional country gardeners did not have access to chemical warfare, but their gardens brimmed with health. Good cultivation and varied planting are the keys to success, and the recognition that every garden actually needs pests because they provide food for other more beneficial insects and small creatures.

A well-tended soil will nourish strong plants, and it is always the weaker specimens that fall prey to pests and diseases, so keep your soil well fed and healthy. Winter maintenance is an important part of pest control — turn over the soil to disturb soil grubs and eggs, bringing them to the surface for birds or cold weather to deal with.

Always choose plants that suit your climate and soil; they have the best chance to thrive and will also look most at home in a country garden. And plant a wide variety of flowering plants to encourage bees and other pollinators, many of which are also important pest killers. Some modern hybrids are more susceptible to pests than traditional varieties of plants, so the choice of variety can also limit pest damage.

Garden friends

Learn to recognize your garden friends. Lacewings are beautiful, delicate insects with translucent pale green wings; aphids are their favorite food. Hover flies are like miniature darting wasps, and skinny, narrow-waisted parasitic wasps lay eggs in soft-bodied insects, mainly caterpillars. The hatching grubs then feed on the bodies of their hosts and kill them. Some of the most efficient pest controllers are tiny larvae that prey on soft-bodied insects, mites, and insect eggs. Lacewing larvae look like miniature greenish gray alligators and not only dispose of aphids but also attack caterpillars and insect larvae, piercing their

Diverse planting keeps your garden healthy. Douglas' meadow foam (Limnanthes douglasii) is one of the best hover fly attractants, and all herbs attract beneficial insects. Nasturtiums are magnets for blackfly, keeping the bugs off more precious plants.

Frog

Hover fly

Ground beetle

Ladybug

PLANTING TO ATTRACT GARDEN FRIENDS

■ Stinging nettles attract a particular species of aphid that provides food for early ladybug and hover fly larvae, which then move on to feast on insect pests elsewhere.

■ To kick-start pest control, make sure you have some early-flowering scented plants such as wallflowers *(Erysimum cheiri)* for early pollinators.

■ All helpful insects like aromatic herbs, so plant borage, hyssop, sages, and lavenders. Grow mints in pots to stop their spreading.

■ A few lavender plants among your roses encourage predators that keep aphids at bay, and a hyssop hedge makes an attractive fragrant edging to vegetables or flowers and will deter imported cabbage moths and caterpillars.

■ Red-flowered buckwheat *(Fagopyron esculentum syn. Polygonum fagopyrum)* is irresistible to hover flies and sits well at the back of a bed, perhaps accompanied by the equally effective and attractive blue-flowering fiddleneck *(Phacelia tanacetiifolia)*.

■ *Convolvulus tricolor* has pretty flowers and is a firm favorite with friendly insects.

■ Fennel, dill, angelica, sweet cicely, and Queen Anne's lace attract lacewings, parasitic wasps, and hover flies.

■ Goldenrod attracts ladybugs and parasitic wasps as well as spiders that consume masses of unwelcome insects.

■ Prince's feather and other amaranths prove magnetic for ladybugs, for shield bugs that gorge on mites, for parasitic wasps, and even shiny, slug-hungry ground beetles.

■ Douglas' meadow foam *(Limnanthes douglasii)* attracts a wide range of insects.

■ Baby blue eyes *(Nemophila menziesii)* and candytuft *(Iberis umbellata)* are favorite plants for adult hover flies.

prey and sucking out their juices. Brownish green hover fly larvae do severe damage to aphid colonies, and tiny grayish ladybug larvae are also voracious. Then the adults come along and continue the killing.

Slugs and snails can be a real nuisance, but a pond, however small, encourages toads and frogs, which eat them. Surround it with plants such as lady's mantle *(Alchemilla mollis)* and hostas that give cool moist shade for ground beetles, which also feast on slugs. Many birds adore snails, so cultivate a bird-friendly garden to provide shelter, water, and food over a long season.

Physical control of pests

You are the most effective pest controller of all. Squash bugs between your fingers, mount evening patrols collecting slugs and snails and drop them into salty water, or spray colonies of aphids with jets of water to dislodge them.

Sometimes you need to devise traps and barriers. If birds are a problem, cover fruit trees and bushes with net, or hang up shiny bird scarers — strips of tinfoil or old CDs are helpful. Cover vegetable crops with floating row cover to keep flying insects off, or hang yellow sticky traps above the rows. You can deter slugs by laying down gritty barriers, remembering to reapply them after rain. Bran, grit, or crushed eggshells can be useful; some country gardeners used to use soot and wood ash, but they can contain small amounts of toxins and are best avoided. You can sink beer traps, renewing them every few days, or place collars of foil or copper wire around plant stems. Cardboard or

carpet underlay collars will protect plants from many soil pests, and cut-off plastic bottles protect vulnerable seedlings — just be careful to remove them in hot weather or young plants will fry.

Rabbits can be a dreadful nuisance in country gardens. The only way to keep them out is to put up a wire fence, burying 12-18 inches (30-45 cm) of the netting firmly in the ground so they can't burrow under it. Wrap sticky tanglefoot-covered bands around fruit tree trunks to stop climbing pests, and hang nuts and balls of fat on their branches in winter to encourage birds to pick off overwintering pests.

Companion planting

All the flowers that attract beneficial insects make good companions, but plants can also provide support in other ways. Some plants produce their own chemical warfare; for example, marigolds *(Tagetes spp.)* excrete substances from their roots that discourage many soil pests; while garlic, onions, and chives excrete enzymes that seem to be actively toxic to many pests.

Aromatic plants can confuse plant-specific pests so it helps to place strongly-scented herbs or onions near cabbages and carrots to keep fleabeetles and carrotflies away. Other scents seem repulsive to pests, particularly rue *(Ruta graveolens)*, wormwood *(Artemisia absinthum)*, and pennyroyal *(Mentha pulegium)*, so plant these at the edge of your vegetable plot, but be careful with rue, which also seems to check the growth of tomatoes and basil.

A few plants are active pest magnets. Nasturtiums lure aphids from beans and some aphids from fruit trees. The common weed sowthistle *(Sonchus olearaceus)* hosts lots of insect pests, so leave some in the vegetable plot then pull them up in early summer, taking numerous bugs along with them.

Some plants help others by providing elements they need. For example, grow beans and peas, which fix nitrogen in the soil, alongside nitrogen-hungry leafy greens. Others offer physical support, protecting vulnerable companions from weather or shading the ground to avoid competitive weed growth. Runner beans will grow up the stems of corn plants and squashes do well in the dappled shade cast by the corn.

Gritty materials such as crushed eggshells will keep slugs off precious young seedlings.

Above: You may need to net strawberries to keep birds off. Keep the nets off the fruit with upended jelly jars on short sticks.

Below: Slugs will congregate under grapefruit skins, but you must lift them each morning and dispose of the pests.

Above: Kale, rocket, peas, chard, beet, and garlic growing in a contented jumble with flowers and herbs.

PLANT DIRECTORY

Choosing plants

Country gardeners are usually a thrifty bunch, originally through necessity, later through intention — why spend money on plants and materials when you can get them for free? The bulk of early country garden plants would have been brought in from the wild or from fields and hedges. Most of them were functional — useful in the country medicine chest or for the kitchen. To these would have been added herbs and flowers gleaned first from monastic gardens, then from the gardens of the "big" houses, and brought back to country gardens by the folk who worked there. So all the plants — fruit, vegetables, herbs, and ornamental flowers — were easy to propagate and share. Because country gardeners didn't usually have a lot of time to spend cosseting plants, the plants also had to be robust and unfussy. Scent was another prized commodity — early country life was not without its odors.

There is no specific definition of a country garden plant because everyone's gardens are so individual, but the plants mentioned in the lists that follow are all easy to propagate, largely trouble-free, disease-resistant, and their flowers have scent wherever possible. Don't fall into the trap of thinking a country garden must be purely traditional and rather static; that's never been the case. Certain ornamental plants have been found to work best for centuries, particularly tall spired flowers and those that spread and ramble, rather than very rigid offerings, but the best country gardens contain a mixture of old and new. Country gardeners have always tried whatever they were able to get their hands on, so do consider including plants that have only recently become widespread. Ornamental grasses, for example, can add just the right touch to a country garden bed, informal and easy to look after, yet striking for a long season. Basically, if you like something, give it a chance. As long as you keep your garden relaxed and unpretentious, you'll enjoy your gardening, and your garden will echo that joy.

Foxgloves and fennel, euphorbia and geraniums, iris and daylilies, achillea and acanthus, salvias and tradescantia — a wonderfully relaxed abundant border where plants have made the space their own.

Heirloom plants

Some common country garden plants have been grown for centuries, keeping a sense of continuity, which is almost reason enough to include them. So-called "heirloom" flowers often have simpler shapes and subtler shades on longer stems than modern versions, so plants are less tidy, and early forms are usually more strongly scented than recent varieties. Older varieties may be hardier and less troubled by pests. Some may seem subdued, others too wanton; but it is worth hanging onto our oldest flowers, not only for their appearance and their history, but because they may contain valuable genetic traits worth preserving.

Early English country gardens were firmly functional, but gardeners have never been able to resist dressing up the basics. As early as the 15th century, Madonna lilies and other flowers would have crept in among the vegetables, with wildflowers such as violets, primroses, periwinkle, foxgloves, and *Rosa gallica* or *Rosa alba*. They joined other natives such as yarrow, monkshood, campanulas, columbine, borage, pennyroyal, tansy, artemisia, mullein, and cranesbill, their places justified as important ingredients in herbal potions. As trade routes opened, foreign plants appeared in grander gardens, and slips of these

Delphiniums and foxgloves

Potentillas and salvias

found their way to country gardens by the mid-16th century. By the end of that century, lavender and clove pinks from southern Europe, fritillaries and tulips from Turkey, lychnis from Russia, daylilies from the Orient, and jasmine from India joined other immigrants such as clematis, Turks-cap lilies, wallflowers, stocks, narcissus, and hyacinths alongside native honeysuckle, dog roses, bachelor's buttons, aquilegias, and other once-wild staples. By the 18th century, most of what we consider common country-garden flowers had arrived, including peonies, alliums, scabious, stocks, and anemones beside the tall spires of hollyhocks, aconites, larkspurs, lupines, fragrant pinks, roses, and sweet peas. If plants were pleasing, they were given a place, and many have stayed popular for centuries, even if their forms have changed with time and fashion.

And it's not only old-fashioned flowers that are worthy of trying. Tasty vegetable varieties have been grown in country gardens since the 1800s and are often far more delicious than modern hybrids. Many of the plants in this directory can be considered heirloom plants and may be labeled so at garden centers and nurseries.

Tulips, pansies, and forget-me-nots

Borage, poppies, and fennel

Perennials

Herbaceous perennials are the mainstay of any country garden — permanent plantings between which you can thread annuals to make the dense but fairly random planting that characterizes the ideal cottage-garden look.

Simple propagation

There are lots of old favorite perennials, handed down through generations largely because they are so easy to propagate — most can be increased by division, which means little more than whacking a fork or spade down the middle of a clump and moving one half. Others need to be increased by cuttings, but this is also much simpler than it sounds: just chop off a leaf stalk or a piece of stem, and root it in potting medium. As long as you make sharp cuts and take cuttings from well-established, healthy plants, pot them up in sterilized medium, and make sure they never dry out, you'll get results. Rose cuttings don't even need potting: just place them in sheltered, sandy trenches outdoors.

Most perennial-bed plants are propagated from softwood cuttings — pieces of the current season's growth. Some with fleshy roots, such as Oriental poppies *(Papaver orientale)*, need to be increased from root cuttings, which are small sections of thick root. Roses are easily increased from cuttings of a woody stem taken soon after the leaves have fallen naturally.

Some perennials — such as species of aquilegias, verbascum, and linaria — increase freely from seed, but will usually try to revert to the dominant species forms, so you'll need to isolate special colored forms. Biennials including foxgloves and hollyhocks reappear year after year from seed once established, so they are listed here with perennials.

The perennials included here form a subjective list rather than an attempt at a comprehensive selection, so you may not find everything you expect. Use it, instead, as a starting point to get an idea of a range of plants that are easy to grow, trouble-free, and easy to propagate. They are also, of course, beautiful.

Spiky heads of echinops have graced gardens for hundreds of years, flowering all summer on upright stems above dense thistle-like leaves.

PROPAGATION

DIVIDING

Many perennial herbaceous plants, herbs, and bulbs can be increased by division. Dig up the clump when the foliage of herbaceous plants and herbs is starting to grow in spring, taking care not to damage the roots. Dig bulbs after they have flowered and leaves have died back.

1 Remove any surplus soil. If fibrous roots are not too matted together, just tease them apart with your fingers and separate them into small pieces of plant **(right)**.

2 Separate large dense clumps by prizing them apart with two forks back to back, or cut solid masses with a knife or spade.

3 Replant the new plants as quickly as possible into well-cultivated, weed-free soil, and water the plants in to settle the soil around their roots.

HARDWOOD CUTTINGS

Hardwood cuttings are used to propagate many woody shrubs including buddleia, forsythia, honeysuckle, privet, and roses. Take hardwood cuttings in late fall and winter when leaves have fallen from the plants.

1 Cut a 12 inch (30 cm) length from a woody shoot, cutting below a leaf joint **(right)**.

2 Trim the top end to just above a leaf joint, and push the cutting to half its depth into a narrow 6 inch (15 cm) deep trench in fertile soil in a sheltered spot in your yard, with a layer of sand in the base to help drainage.

3 Settle the soil firmly around the cuttings, keep them well watered and dig up new plants the following fall.

SOFTWOOD CUTTINGS

Softwood cuttings are the most reliable way of propagating most shrubs and herbs. Take cuttings from the current year's growth in late spring or early summer when the shoots are soft but not floppy and before the stem gets hard and woody.

1 Cut the shoot just below a leaf node **(right)**, taking a cutting 2-4 inches (5-10 cm) long.

2 Cut off any lower leaves and insert the stem about 1 inch (2.5 cm) into moist potting medium mixed with sand. The newer and fresher the growth from where you took the cutting, the faster it will root, so always take cuttings from healthy vigorous shoots and keep them in a sealed plastic bag until you are ready to put them into the medium.

ROOT CUTTINGS

Plants with fleshy roots, such as Oriental poppies, can be propagated from root cuttings.

1 Carefully dig up the plant when it is dormant, cut off one or two thick roots; then return the parent plant to its place. With a sharp knife, cut the roots carefully into short 2-3 inch (5-7.5 cm) lengths, slicing them straight across at the top end and angled at the base **(right)**.

2 Insert the cuttings into a pot of moist potting medium mixed with sand. Cuttings should root and sprout within four to six months.

TOP TEN PERENNIALS FOR A SUNNY BED

Anthemis cupaniana

Artemisia spp.

Cynara cardunculus

Dianthus spp.

Echinops ritro

Iris florentina

Kniphofia spp.

Monarda didyma

Nepeta x faassenii

Penstemon spp.

TOP TEN PERENNIALS FOR SHADE OR SEMI-SHADE

Acanthus mollis latifolius

Alchemilla mollis

Convallaria majalis

Digitalis lutea

Geranium phaeum

Helleborus niger

Hesperis matronalis

Hosta spp.

Polygonatum spp.

Pulmonaria spp.

TOP TEN PERENNIALS FOR ARID CONDITIONS

Achillea spp.

Catananche caerulea

Centaurea cyanus

Diascia 'Blackthorn Apricot'

Euphorbia myrsinites

Linaria purpurea

Sedum spectabile

Sisyrinchium californicum

Stachys lanata

Verbascum chaixii

Acanthus mollis
ACANTHUS, BEAR'S BREECHES
Height 5 ft/1.5 m, Spread 3 ft/1 m

A large dramatic plant for the back of a bed, acanthus was known to medieval herbalists in southern Europe as brank-ursine, and was used for a variety of purposes including soothing burns. Usually grown primarily for its stature and glossy, deeply cut leaves rather like exaggerated thistle leaves; generous greenish-purple flower bracts emerge in late summer. Acanthus will grow in sun or partial shade in well-drained soil and can be easily propagated by seed sown in early summer or division of its long thonglike roots in late winter. It can be a touch invasive in a small garden, but sometimes large dramatic plants can make a small space seem larger, as long as you don't crowd them too much. *A. spinosus* flowers very freely in full sun, above very finely cut leaves.

Achillea spp.
YARROW
Height 2-4 ft/60-120 cm, Spread 18 in./45 cm

Named after Achilles, who is said to have used the plant to staunch his warrior's wounds on the battlefield, there is a wide range of achilleas with grayish fernlike foliage and wide flat-topped heads of small square-petaled daisylike flowers in midsummer. *A. ptarmica* 'The Pearl' is an old variety known as shirtbuttons, with clusters of white buttonlike flowers from midsummer through fall. *A.* 'Moonshine' is 24 inches (60 cm) tall with generous silvery foliage and erect stems bearing milky-yellow flower heads that last for many weeks from late summer, and are good for drying. *A.* 'Salmon Beauty' grows to 3 feet (1 m), producing pale salmon pink flowerheads fading to creamy yellow. Increase plants by division in spring.

Aconitum napellus
MONKSHOOD OR WOLFSBANE
Height 4 ft/120 cm, Spread 12 in./30 cm

Native to Europe's damp woods and hedges, monkshood is a characteristic country-garden plant with rich green, deeply cut, feathery foliage and tapering spires of hooded, helmet-shaped, inky blue flowers in midsummer. The graceful white-flowered form *A. napellus* 'Album' is a good old-fashioned plant. *A.* 'Bressingham Spire' has deep violet flowers. *A. x cammarum* 'Bicolor' produces short dense spikes of violet blue and white flowers. The plant was allegedly a crucial ingredient in medieval witches' flying potion (along with deadly nightshade and henbane), and the roots of monkshoods are poisonous, so be careful when planting and dividing them. Wearing gloves will help you to avoid getting contact dermatitis when handling monkshoods. But they are a must for any sunny or semi-shady bed with moist soil, and a magnet for bees and other helpful insects. You'll get a second flush of flowers in early fall if you cut the first blooms back in time. Sow seed in the fall.

Alcea spp.
HOLLYHOCKS
Height 7 ft/2.25 m, Spread 3 ft/1 m

Everyone associates hollyhocks with country gardens, and rightly so: they have been part of the scene since the 16th century, reaching peak popularity in the early 19th century when at least 90 named varieties were available — single-, double-, and pompom-flowered ones. However, most older varieties succumbed to rust, and the choice of reliable modern biennial hollyhocks is much narrower. Grow them in your beds, or by a gate or front door, where you will appreciate their towering spires of papery flowers in mid to late summer. Most modern varieties are reasonably rust-resistant, but a bit of rust doesn't really matter if the foliage is largely disguised by other plants. It's the spires of flowers that catch the eye. *A. rugosa* has tall spires with peach and yellow flowers and deeply lobed, rust-resistant leaves. *A. ficifolia*, the fig-leaved hollyhock, is another popular, reliable, yellow or orange-flowered form. *A. rosea* 'Nigra' was first cultivated around the beginning of the 18th century, producing gleaming purple-black waxy flowers. Sow hollyhock seed in the fall.

Alchemilla mollis

LADY'S MANTLE

Height 12 in./30 cm, Spreads readily

A beautiful foliage plant, with its fresh acid-green leaves that trap drops of dew and rain, leaving them sparkling in jewel-like spheres in the fluted foliage. It's one of those plants that will grow anywhere, sun or shade, poor or rich soil, and it self-seeds to spring up in cracks in paving, in gravel, and wherever there's a gap — but it's not difficult to pull up if you really feel the need. Perfect to spill over the edge of a path or steps, it perhaps looks its best in shade and in the early morning with the dew still on it. In midsummer it produces sprays of lime green starry flowers that are a stunning foil to lavender. If you want to stop it from spreading prolifically, snip off the flowerheads before they set seed, or plant the less vigorous species, *A. conjuncta,* which has blue-green leaves with silky gray undersides.

Anchusa azurea

Height 3-5 ft/1-1.5 m, Spread 24 in./60 cm

This erect, clump-forming perennial has tall spires of blue-purple starry flowers above hairy, lance-shaped dark green leaves. Some varieties can be a little invasive, but every garden should include *A. azurea* 'Loddon Royalist' which flowers in early summer, its gentian blue flowers and sturdy stems a perfect foil to pink and purple Oriental poppies. It likes sun but is not fussy about soil type and can be increased by root cuttings or sowing seed in spring.

Anemone x hybrida spp.

JAPANESE ANEMONE

Height 4 ft/120 cm, Spreads vigorously

Perfect for late summer flowering, the delicate saucer-shaped pink and white single flowers of the Japanese anemone bloom well into fall in any fertile soil in sun or partial shade. Excellent to take beds into winter or in shady plantings with cyclamen and autumn crocus. *A. x hybrida* 'Honorine Jobert' has shallow white flowers with yellow and green centers above the characteristic serrated leaves, while the almost

evergreen *A. hupehensis* has deeply divided leaves and white or purplish pink blossoms with darker reverse petals. The only problem with Japanese anemones is that they grow vigorously, so plant them with care and divide them each winter if you're short of space in the flower bed.

Anthemis punctata sssp. cupaniana

Height 12 in./30 cm, Spread 24 in./60cm

Once established, this cheerful daisy flowers from spring until midwinter. White flowers with yellow centers are continuously produced on fine, lax, gray stems above feathery cut gray leaves. Happy in fairly miserable soils in sun or semi-shade, this plant makes a useful edging or gap filler, and in warm yards, the leaves stay grayish green all winter. Though plants can be tender, they are incredibly easy to reproduce; just snip off a stem and it will root in water within a matter of days. Taller at about 3 feet (1 m), the golden marguerite *(A. tinctoria)* produces brilliant yellow daisies in summer above mats of green foliage and is happy flopping near the front of a bed, while the similarly sized *A. tinctoria* 'Grallach Gold' has a mass of acid-yellow daisy flowers on more upright stems for several months from early summer onward.

Aquilegia vulgaris

COLUMBINE, BONNETS

Height 2-3 ft/60-90 cm, Spread 12-18 in./ 30-45 cm

Aquilegias are a favorite country garden plant. Their divided, rounded, blue-green leaves emerge cheerfully in early spring before much else gets going; then from late spring into early summer, gloriously delicate, graceful flowers with long spurs and a wide range of faces from helmets to pompoms and intricate Origami-style bells float above the beds. *A. vulgaris* 'Nora Barlow' is a beautiful old-fashioned variety that spreads happily with very double or pompom-style red, white, or pink flowers, often edged in green. *A. canadensis* has red

Alcea rosea

Anchusa azurea 'Loddon Royalist'

Aquilegia 'Nora Barlow'

and yellow flowers and dark green foliage, and there are dozens of attractive hybrids in a wide choice of colors, but they won't come true to seed because *A. vulgaris* is terrifically promiscuous and crosses with all its relatives to attempt to transform even the most vivid color combination to something resembling its native purple. But the results are often charming and surprising, and it is a joy to let aquilegias spread themselves through your beds with abandon.

Artemisia spp.
SOUTHERNWOOD
Height and Spread 30 in./75 cm
This huge family of aromatic silver-gray leaved perennials is grown for its foliage — their flowers are fairly insignificant. Originating from the Mediterranean, they need well-drained soil and tolerate dry conditions but not wet feet. *A.* 'Powis Castle' produces a mound of very finely cut silvery foliage and sprays of small yellow flowerheads in midsummer; *A. ludoviciana* is a shorter (16 in./40 cm) bushy perennial grown principally for its very aromatic lance-shaped woolly silver leaves.

Astrantia major
MASTERWORT
Height 2 ft/60 cm, Spread 18 in./45 cm
This trouble-free old country-garden plant grows happily in sun or partial shade, providing long-lasting clumps of spiky greenish white papery flowers with a pale green collar on straight, stiff stems. *A. major* 'Shaggy' is particularly good; 'Rubra' has delectable red flowers; and the stunning blood red *A. major* 'Hadspen Blood' looks magnificent in almost any situation, but is slightly smaller (height and spread 12 in./30 cm) and less prolific than the other varieties.

Campanula spp.
BELLFLOWERS, CANTERBURY BELLS
Height and Spread vary
Old-fashioned country perennials known for their simple blue and white bell-shaped flowers in early and midsummer. There are all sorts of sizes and habits, from the invaluable edging of sprawling, low (4 in./10 cm) *Campanula carpatica*, which spreads its starry sky-blue flowers happily in sun or partial shade, to the sun-loving, tall *C. lactiflora* (height 5 ft/1.5 m,

spread 2 ft/60 cm) which flowers all summer in a sunny position with tall spires of lilac bellflowers. *C. latifolia* is another good tall variety (height 4 ft/120 cm, spread 2 ft/60 cm), a prolifically self-seeding old British native with blue, violet, or white flowers. *C. pyramidalis*, the chimney bellflower, is another traditional variety, but needs a very sunny spot and because it is short-lived, best treated as a biennial or resown each fall. It reaches 5 feet (1.5 m) with huge spikes of cup-shaped flowers. *C. glomerata* 'Crown of Snow' is an attractive white form (height 2 ft/60 cm) of the British bellflower, producing large clusters of white flowers throughout summer.

Cardamine pratensis
LADY'S SMOCK
Height 8 in./20 cm
Not really a bedding plant, but if you have a shady damp spot, or an area of rough grass, be sure to plant lady's smock, which will naturalize happily if it likes the conditions. Small pink or white flowers arrive in spring, and you occasionally come across the rare and beautiful double form *C. pratensis flore pleno*.

Centaurea montana

Centranthus ruber

Convallaria majalis

Catananche caerulea

Height 2 ft/60 cm, Spread 12 in./30 cm

Another easy plant for any sunny garden. All summer, small papery everlasting-type flowers of deep blue sit on top of wiry stems emerging from a neat clump of grassy stems. Plants can be slightly tender, particularly 'Bicolor', which is white with blue centers, so provide a sheltered position and well-drained soil.

Centaurea spp.

PERENNIAL BACHELOR'S BUTTONS, KNAPWEED, CORNFLOWER

Height and Spread vary

Reliable, no-fuss perennials with gray-green, lance-shaped leaves and thistle-shaped flower heads. They thrive in sun in any but the wettest soil, flowering from late spring to midsummer as long as they are regularly deadheaded. The vigorous *C. montana* is the most common (height 16 in./40cm) with its bright blue flowers, but sadly the beautiful white form *C. montana alba*, with its black centers, is much less prolific. Purple-headed *C. cyanus* (16 in./40 cm), or knapweed, makes a good country-garden plant, and the taller (2 ft/60 cm) clump-forming *C. hypoleuca* 'John Coutts' makes a fine show of bright pink heads.

Centranthus ruber

VALERIAN

Height 2-3 ft/60-90 cm, Spread 18 in./45 cm

A popular country plant that likes poor chalky soil and a sunny spot, and is often found growing enthusiastically on walls and old steps. The large heads of small reddish pink or white flowers are very popular with bees and other insects, but if valerian likes your yard, you'll have to control it quite rigidly or it will try to take over.

Cephalaria gigantea

GIANT SCABIOUS

Height 6 ft 6 in./2 m, Spread 5 ft/1.5 m

This robust, summer-flowering, giant-headed scabious has large primrose-yellow pincushion flowers on upright hairy stems in midsummer.

It looks most at home at the back of a bed, but will need staking in a windy spot, and you must divide clumps every three years or so to prevent it from spreading too wildly.

Cerastium tomentosum

SNOW IN SUMMER

Height 4 in./10 cm, Spread 8 in./20 cm

An invaluable edging plant with small white or blue bells that peer skyward out of mats of green foliage. It needs warmth and a light soil to keep it flowering all summer.

Cirsium rivulare atropurpureum

Height 4 ft/120 cm, Spread 3 ft/1 m

This airy plant produces striking crimson pincushions like miniature thistles on tall branching stems in early to midsummer, and will flower again in early fall if it is cut back promptly after the first flush of flowers. Another sun-loving plant, it prefers fairly rich soil.

Convallaria majalis

LILY-OF-THE-VALLEY

Height 8 in./20 cm, Spread 12-24 in./30-60 cm

The sweet, delicate scent of lily-of-the-valley is pure nostalgia, and everyone should try to include this little plant in their gardens. Once established it will spread and you'll be giving roots to anyone who'll take them after a few years, but in some situations it just refuses to shift. In theory it will grow in any soil in sun or shade, but it balks at deep shade and heavy clay. A good form is the large-flowered *C. majalis* 'Fortin's Giant', and *C. majalis* var. *rosea* has pretty pale pink bells.

Cynara cardunculus

ORNAMENTAL ARTICHOKE

Height and Spread 6 ft 6 in./2 m

A very statuesque plant, this makes a striking structural piece among more relaxed forms of other country-garden perennials, and it thrives in a sunny spot in any rich, moist soil, even the heaviest clay. Distinctive spiky silvery leaves arch out of a thick gray stem, topped in summer

with artichoke heads that eventually open into violet-blue thistlelike flowers. Plants need to be staked and divided in spring. Cut them back before hard frost, and cover the stems with a mulch of straw or leaves for winter.

Delphinium spp.

Height 3 ft-8 ft/1-2.4 m, Spread 3 ft/1 m

The tall spires of blue, white, and pink delphiniums instantly spring to mind when you think of country-garden plants, and they are as much a part of the scene as hollyhocks and foxgloves, although the hybrids we grow today were first bred in the 1870s and are in fact comparative newcomers in terms of plant history. You can find varieties to suit most tastes, in all shades from very deep blue through pink to white, but all need a sunny, open site with free-draining soil, and you must stake taller varieties. If the flower stalks are cut back immediately after flowering, you will get two flowerings each year, and regular cutting encourages lateral growth and bushy plants. Slugs and delphiniums go hand in hand, so protect seedlings in spring with cloches or barriers of gritty material. New plants raised from root cuttings seem less vulnerable than seedlings sown the previous fall.

Dianthus spp.

PINKS

Height and Spread 12-18 in./30-45 cm

Another evocative species, old-fashioned pinks have heady clovelike scents and fringed flowers that have been enjoyed for many centuries. With sun, good drainage, and a reasonably alkaline soil, they will happily spread to form generous silvery-leaved clumps with masses of delightful long-lasting summer flowers in shades of red, pink, and white with wonderful markings and superb perfume. All are ideal for the front of sunny beds, but they do need good drainage. 'Mrs Sinkins' has richly scented double white fringed flowers; 'Sops-in-Wine' is another old variety with crimson flowers blotched with white. 'Fair Folly' is clove scented with dusky pink flowers splashed with white. Although their scents are rarely quite as strong, modern hybrids produce flowers throughout the summer if they are dead headed regularly. 'Gran's Favourite' is white laced with purple. 'Doris' is an excellent double pale pink variety, with red rings. Don't be persuaded to buy any of the many modern varieties without scent. Pinks are easily propagated by cuttings from late spring to midsummer.

Dianthus barbatus
SWEET WILLIAM
Height and Spread 8-24 in./20-60 cm
Another old favorite, strongly scented and nostalgic, dianthus is biennial and flowers in midsummer for only a few weeks, so its place is often taken by stronger, showier plants. Nevertheless, try to find room for a few clumps of these charming plants with their knock-out scent and velvety, lacy flowers.

Diascia spp.
Height 10 in./25 cm, Spread 20 in./50 cm
Among this family of annuals and perennials are some stunners for very dry sunny gardens. Given the right conditions they will produce loose spires or clusters of largely pink-toned flowers above delicate heart-shaped leaves from early summer into fall as long as you keep dead-heading. *D.* 'Blackthorn Apricot' has loose heads of pale apricot flowers; *D.* 'Rupert Lambert' has double deep pink flowers.

Dicentra spectabilis
BLEEDING HEARTS/DUTCHMAN'S BREECHES
Height 2 ft/60 cm, Spread 18 in./45 cm
Another favorite. White-tipped red hearts dangle from graceful arching stems from late spring into midsummer. They provide welcome early color and height when most other perennials are scarcely awake, and have attractive ferny foliage. They shine out from shady places, growing well in fairly deep shade as long as the soil is rich and moisture retentive. The white *D. spectabilis alba* is slightly more temperamental to establish, but worth the effort.

Digitalis spp.
FOXGLOVES
Height 3-5 ft/1-1.5 m, Spreads readily
Foxgloves have been appearing in country gardens since earliest times. Spires of bell-shaped flowers can be found in pink, purple, white, and yellow, many with attractive speckled throats above generous, slightly felted green leaves. All foxgloves like semi-shade and a moist humus-rich soil, but once established they seed themselves happily in most conditions. They are biennials; don't be depressed when a marvelous display one year fails to reappear. Instead, sow or plant them in alternate years to get clumps established. The one caveat is that they don't grow happily for everybody, and if you really have difficulties getting them going, forget them and plant something more willing. *D. lutea* is a neat form of the native British foxglove, producing clumps of upright spires with hanging creamy yellow bells among oval mid-green leaves. *D. ferruginea* has dark green leaves, tall flower stems, coppery trumpet-shaped flowers veined in brown, and attractive seedheads.

Echinacea purpurea
CONEFLOWER
Height 4 ft/1.2 m, Spread 18 in./45 cm
A North American native, coneflowers produce large purple-pink or white heads of daisylike flowers with deep brown centers. Also grown on a large scale for many herbal preparations, they make striking and easy country-garden plants, flowering from midsummer into fall. They are sometimes a little reluctant their first year, but thereafter flower prolifically in sun and well-drained soil. Increase them by sowing seed in the fall or take root cuttings.

Echinops spp.
GLOBE THISTLE
Height 4 ft/120 cm, Spread 2 ft/60 cm
Upright and clump forming, *Echinops ritro* has jagged, dark green thistlelike foliage and steely blue flower balls from late summer well into fall on strong spikes that don't need staking. *E. ritro* 'Veitch's Blue' has tight purplish blue flowers. *E. ritro* subsp. *ruthenicus* has a slightly neater habit, shiny green foliage with a silvery sheen, and strong, deep blue flowerheads. As with so

Echinacea purpurea

Echinops ritro

many perennials, the white forms seem slightly less resilient, but they are generally trouble free if they are planted in full sun and rich soil. They can succumb to aphids, so plant nasturtiums somewhere nearby to lure the pests away.

Erysimum spp.
WALLFLOWERS
Height and Spread 12-18 in./30-45 cm
Biennial wallflowers still appear in most country gardens in Europe where they provide masses of small scented blossoms early in spring. Early-flowering varieties attract early pollinators and beneficial insects to give a head start in your garden; for this reason they were once widely grown around fruit trees. They thrive in sunny positions in any well-drained soil, and once they are established they are willing colonizers of tumbledown walls and old paths. *Erysimum* 'Bowles Mauve' is a vigorous, old-fashioned, evergreen form with narrow gray-green leaves and fragrant mauve flowers from late winter to summer. *E.* 'Harpur Crewe' is another old favorite, producing intensely fragrant double and semi-double yellow flowers from late spring through summer over stiff evergreen foliage.

Euphorbia spp.
SPURGES
Height and Spread vary
This large group of shrubby plants encompasses many shapes, sizes, and forms. Plant *E. palustris* (height and spread 3ft/1m) for a grand splash of yellow in spring, followed by green plumes of flowers all summer, which turn yellow and orange in the fall. Look out for evergreen *E. characias* subsp. *wulfenii* (height and spread 4ft/120cm) with tall spikes of full greenish yellow cylindrical flowers above lime green foliage in early spring. They grow well in sun or semi-shade in well-drained soils, whereas the useful prostate form *E. myrsinites*, with waxy blue-green leaves and large lime green flowers in spring, needs a very dry spot in full sun. *E. polychroma* (height and spread 18 in./45 cm) has lime green flowers above a dome of bright green foliage in early summer and

will tolerate semi-shade, and the bushy *E. palustris* (height and spread 2 ft/60 cm) has lime yellow flowers through summer and good yellow and orange fall foliage; it needs semi-shade and moist soil. Always wear gloves when tending spurges: many people have an allergic reaction — contact dermatitis — to the plants' milky sap.

Galega orientalis
GOAT'S RUE
Height 4 ft/1.2 m, Spread 24 in./60 cm
Subtle rather than showy pealike violet flowers rise above divided foliage in summer, but free-flowering goat's rue is very attractive in a sunny position in the middle of a mixed bed among more obvious blooms. It is rather lax and needs to be staked or supported with more upright neighboring plants. *G. orientalis* 'Alba' is a popular white variety. *G.* x *hartlandii* 'His Majesty' has lilac and white flowers above lance-shaped leaves of oval leaflets.

Geranium spp.
GERANIUMS
Height and Spread vary

Incredibly useful plants, there is a huge choice of geraniums, from those that form soft clumps at different heights, to those that sprawl over and through other plants. The wild form *G. pratense* or cranesbill (height 2-3 ft/60-90 cm, spread 2 ft/60 cm) was grown by the earliest country gardeners and is still a valuable addition to a perennial bed, with relaxed mounds of purple flowers through summer. Dusky cranesbill (*G. phaeum*), (height 30 in./75 cm, spread 18 in./45 cm), with its white-centered, purple flowers is a marvelous shade-loving perennial. But there are dozens if not hundreds of varieties to choose from, all easy to grow in any well-drained soil, in sun or partial shade. *G.* 'Johnson's Blue' is rightly popular, forming mounds 12 inches (30 cm) tall and 2 feet (60 cm) across with good blue flowers veined in darker blue in early summer. *G. macrorrhizum* has a similar habit but produces a mass of pink flowers in spring, and leaves turn bronze and often remain on the plants all winter. *G. maculatum* is a popular 2 feet (60 cm) tall, mound-forming geranium, with very soft foliage topped with a mass of

Galega orientalis

Geranium psilostemon

Helleborus orientalis

Hosta sieboldiana var. elegans, with Linaria purpurea in background

lilac flowers. *G. renardii* is a very neat plant about 8 inches (20 cm) tall with gray felted, scallop-edged leaves and white flowers threaded with faint purple veins.

Geum rivale
AVENS
Height and Spread 12 in./30 cm
Clumps of rather coarse, dark green, lobed foliage support long, fine stems topped with delicate, slightly drooping, pinkish brown, rounded flowers in early summer. Happy in well-drained soils in sun or partial shade. An understandable favorite, *G.* 'Mrs Bradshaw' with scarlet flowers in small sprays and bright green leaves, makes a very bright spot in any bed. *G.* 'Lady Stratheden' is a good deep yellow form.

Helleborus spp.
CHRISTMAS ROSE
Height 12-24 in./30-60 cm, Spread 18 in.-3 ft/ 45 cm-1 m
There are many hellebores, all grown in moist, shady spots for their winter and spring flowers. One of the largest, *H. argutifolius* is an old-fashioned, spreading, bushy woodland plant with leathery green foliage and green bell flowers. The Lenten rose *(H. orientalis)* is more striking, growing to 18 inches (45 cm) tall. Its cup-shaped flowers in white, pink, or purple are sometimes spotted in contrasting colors and flower in early spring. It follows hard on the heels of *Helleborus niger,* the smaller Christmas rose, with its cup-shaped white flowers with gold stamens and deepest green foliage. Unfortunately, it rarely blossoms happily by Christmas but is a joyous sight in late winter. Give hellebores space, be patient, and don't disturb them.

Hemerocallis spp.
DAYLILIES
Height and Spread 18 in.-3 ft/45 cm-1 m
Today, robust hybrid daylilies come in a wide variety of colors, shapes, and sizes to suit all tastes and are an essential part of a country flowerbed. They form generous clumps with deep green foliage and lily flowers that last one day. Flowers are produced in succession for several weeks in spring and summer. Grow them in moist, humus-rich, and well-drained soil in full sun. Favorites include the small (18 in./ 45 cm) *H.* 'Scarlet Orbit' with midsummer flowers in rich scarlet and gold with green throats, and *H.* 'Starling' with purplish brown 26-inch (70 cm) tall flowers in late spring, but there are excellent hybrids to choose from.

Hesperis matronalis
SWEET ROCKET
Height 18-24 in./45-60 cm
This traditional country plant flowers in May and is lovely with late tulips. A froth of white or pale pink scented flowers lasts for weeks above branching stems, growing happily in any soil, and in semi-shade. They are most vigorous on alkaline soil where they will seed themselves freely around the beds. The white double form *H. matronalis flore pleno* is worth searching out.

Hosta spp.
HOSTAS
Height and Spread 1-3 ft/25 cm-1 m
Although handy, hostas are not traditional country garden plants. Their distinctive, generous, ribbed leaves are irresistible if you have a shady area with rich well-drained soil and make a terrific foil for more old-fashioned plants. The substantial (height and spread 3 ft/ 1 m) *H. montana aureomarginata* is worth growing for its dark green veined leaves with gold margins, with pale violet flowers above the foliage in midsummer. Similarly generous *H. sieboldiana* 'Frances Williams' has large blue-gray heart-shaped leaves with an irregular yellowish edge, and the smaller *H.* 'Hadspen Blue' (height 10 in./25 cm and spread 24 in./ 50 cm) with small heart-shaped blue-green leaves, is easy to fit into smaller spaces. Slugs and snails love hostas, so protect their emerging leaves in spring with gritty barriers, but if they are too problematic, give the space to something easier.

Iris spp.
IRIS
Height and Spread vary

Irises have been grown in European country gardens for centuries. They are easy to cultivate in sunny positions and increase happily. Among the 400 or so species that grow in the northern hemisphere, traditional *Iris florentina* (height 2 ft/60 cm, spread 12 in./30 cm) is a must for any dry, sunny country-garden bed with its sweetly scented blue-gray flowers above sword-shaped leaves. Another traditional plant is the stinking iris, *(I. foetidissima)* (height and spread 18 in./45 cm), worth growing for its vivid decorative seed pods, which split in the fall to reveal orange-red seeds. *I. sibirica,* the fine-leaved water iris (height 3 ft/1 m and spread 10 in./25 cm), is another traditional iris that has spawned many varieties, including the beautiful *I. sibirica* 'Perrys Blue' with striking dark blue flowers. These grow best in a boggy but sunny situation, as does sweet flag *(I. pallida),* another ancient plant, with fragrant lilac-blue flowers in early summer. *I. pallida* 'Dalmatica' is an attractive heirloom form with soft blue, scented flowers with yellow beards. Divide iris every three or four years by splitting off young rhizomes with leaves attached and replanting them just under the soil.

Knautia macedonica
PINCUSHION FLOWER
Height 30 in./75 cm, Spread 3 ft/1 m

A fantastic value plant, producing small deep red, scabious-type flowers on gently branching stems from spring to fall. They are wonderful for gently rambling through neighboring plants or near the front of a bed, because they are one of those delightful see-through plants that add to anything planted nearby rather than intruding or blocking it. Grow them in any well-drained soil in a sunny site.

Kniphofia
RED-HOT POKER
Height 5 ft/1.5 m, Spread 2 ft/60 cm

Red-hot pokers have been grown for 150 years in country gardens, their stiff red spiky blooms striking in late summer. They fell out of fashion for a while, probably because of their rigid upright habit which some people found hard to place, but they are cheerful plants. You can find all sorts of smaller, attractive hybrids, but if you have space, try old-fashioned *K. uvaria* with its autumnal pokers of bright pink, changing to red, orange, and finally greenish yellow. Plant in a sunny spot in well manured and well-drained soil for best results, and disguise their rather messy foliage with other plantings.

Linaria purpurea
Height 36 in./90 cm, Spread 12 in./30 cm

Once you've planted linaria, you've probably got it forever because it self seeds freely around your yard, flowering from early summer to fall in light soils in reasonably sunny positions. Some people consider it a bit of a weed, but the slender stems, graceful linear foliage, and spires of deep purple flowers are extremely welcome additions to many gardens. If it does crop up in the wrong place (and it will), it's easy enough to get rid of it since it's not deep rooting, but you'll probably get to love it. The more sought after version is *L. purpurea* 'Canon Went' with pale pink flowers and darker foliage, but this will only come true to seed if it's isolated from the purple-flowered species.

Linum narbonense
FLAX
Height 2 ft/60 cm, Spread 18 in./45 cm

This easy plant dances like small blue butterflies through the front of a bed, producing masses of pale azure-blue, open flowers during summer above very fine stems and delicate leaves. Plant in a well-drained, sunny situation — the flowers close up in shade or on cloudy days — and propagate from cuttings in summer.

Lupinus spp.
LUPINES
Height 4 ft/120 cm, Spread 2 ft/60 cm

Another staple for any country garden, the traditional lupine *(Lupinus polyphyllus)* has largely been superceded by 20th-century Russell hybrid lupines with their tall spires plump with pealike blossoms in a wide range of colors in early summer. They need a sunny spot and rich soil. The down sides of lupines are that their flowering period is short, slugs love them, and they can succumb to mildew. However, there is still something irresistible about them; cut the spires back immediately after flowering for a second show of blooms.

Lychnis spp.
ROSE CAMPION
Height 3 ft/1 m, Spread 18 in./45 cm

Far from subtle, the bright cerise-pink open flowers of rose campion *(Lychnis coronaria)* make perfect splashes of vivid color in a country flowerbed in high summer. The gray felty leaves are attractive, too, and the tall, wiry, branching stems make it an easy plant to place because you can see through it. Preferring sun and dry soil, there is also a white form, but do try the pink form. *Lychnis chalcedonica,* Maltese Cross, is a brilliantly scarlet member of the family with green foliage and stouter stems. It is named because it is supposed to have been taken home to Britain by Crusaders in the 11th century. *L. × arkwrightii* 'Vesuvius' is more compact (height 18 in./45 cm, spread 12 in./30 cm) with orange flowers in late summer.

Meconopsis betonicifolia
HIMALAYAN POPPY
Height 18-24 in./45-60 cm, Spread 2 ft/60 cm

Try these poppies if you have a cool, moist, and shady area of yard. Their clusters of sky blue, papery poppies are a joy in early summer, and they have attractively sturdy stems and mid-green foliage. But if they don't succeed for you, plant something else. They can be terribly temperamental, and even when established are short-lived plants. They must be propagated from seed sown in summer. However, their relative *Meconopsis cambrica,* the Welsh poppy (height 12-18 in./30-45 cm), is much more easy-going. Cheerful yellow and orange flowers appear above ferny foliage from early summer for many weeks, joyfully blossoming in shade or sun in any but the wettest soil, and self-seeding with abandon.

Monarda didyma
BEE BALM, BERGAMOT
Height 3 ft/1.2 m, Spread 18 in./45 cm

Bee balm is a native of North America, and in the 18th century, it was taken to Britain where it became a country-garden favorite for the back of the bed, with its clusters of hooded red flowers on long stems. It has an unkempt habit and tends to flop, so it needs to be supported with stiffer plants, but it's worth including for its excellent color and because it is a bee and insect magnet, vital in any chemical-free war against pests. Grow in rich, moisture-retentive soil in a sunny situation. *Monarda* 'Cambridge Scarlet' is an old variety with rich red flowers and aromatic leaves. The taller (3 ft 9 in./1.4 m) *M. fistulosa* 'Scorpio' has deep purplish pink flowers and is happy in dry soil.

Nepeta spp.
CATNIP
Height and Spread vary

One of the best value of all country-garden plants, catnip forms a mound of gray-blue, aromatic, toothed-leaved stems with clusters of lavender-blue flowers all summer. Perfect for the front of beds or cascading over a terrace or wall where larger forms can sprawl. Catnip likes warm dry conditions, particularly in chalky soil. Cut it back hard in midsummer to encourage a second long period of flowering, and divide clumps in the late fall – though a single stem of catnip will root quite happily in the ground or in a glass of water. *N. × faassenii* is the most compact variety (Height and spread 18 in./45 cm), ideal for edging beds and paths. *N.* 'Six Hills Giant' is a taller, tougher version (height and spread 3 ft/1 m). *N. govaniana* is an unusual 3 foot (1 m) variety that likes partial shade and more moisture, and produces long panicles of creamy white flowers in late summer. Bees, butterflies, insects, and cats love it.

Paeonia spp.
PEONY
Height and Spread 2-3 ft/60-90 cm

Grown in European country gardens for a millennium, peonies are gloriously sumptuous.

Their huge round buds above shiny dark green foliage, often tinged with red, offer great promise in spring. Buds open into voluptuous flowers in early summer. *P. officinalis* is the native British species; among its many pink, red, and white single and double varieties, *P. officinalis* 'Crimson Globe' has magnificent double crimson flowers. *P. lactiflora*, also known as the Chinese peony, flowers in early summer with a large, white, single flower with yellow stamens and red foliage. *P. lactiflora* 'Edulis Superba' is an early-blooming double pink cultivar, while *P. lactiflora* 'Sarah Bernhardt' produces a mass of large tissue-pink blooms in midsummer. Peonies need sun and rich soil, and like to be kept moist. They are generally slow to get going, and if they are moved once they are established, they will sulk for several seasons before grudgingly flowering once again.

Papaver orientale
ORIENTAL POPPY
Height 2 ft 6 in.-4 ft/75-120 cm, Spread 3 ft/90 cm

Easy to grow, with huge showy flowers in

Meconopsis betonicifolia

Phlox paniculata 'Prospero'

Candelabra primrose Primula florindae

stunning colors, these are real come-hither plants, demanding the attention of all who glimpse them, yet almost thriving on neglect. They like any well-drained soil in a sunny position, but will tolerate semi-shade. They flower through early summer, then collapse into midsummer slovenliness, so make sure other summer favorites such as delphiniums and phlox are ready to blossom in front of them. A traditional country plant, the bright red *P. orientale,* is wonderful in the vegetable patch, serenading emerging vegetables. Another favorite in this seductive family is *P. orientale* 'Patty's Plum', the flowers voluptuous confections of crumpled crepe paper, smoky purplish mauve around a deep purple eye with delicate brush marks of black at the base, fading to wrapping-paper brown before each blossom drops. 'Cedric Morris' is another beautiful variety with very frilly flesh-pink petals surrounding huge black doelike eyes. Or try 'Perry's White', a clear white with a burgundy central blotch and deepest purple anthers. Increase by division or root cuttings.

Penstemon spp.
PENSTEMON
There are more than 250 species of penstemon native to North and Central America, but this flower has always been particularly favored in Britain. Very easy plants, they boast attractive clusters of tubular flowers on long stems, and contrary to popular belief they tolerate even severely cold weather as long as their feet aren't wet. They need to be cut back to tidy up straggly growth after the last frost. Provide them with a well-drained sunny site and they'll flourish. *P. barbatus* (height 3 ft/1 m, spread 12 in./30 cm) bears spikes of bright scarlet flowers, often with pink throats. *P.* 'Blackbird' (height 2 ft/60 cm, spread 12 in./30 cm) has dark maroon flowers all summer. *P.* 'Evelyn' (height 15 in./40 cm, spread 8 in./20 cm) has salmon pink flowers with cream throats. All species are easy to propagate from soft cuttings in late summer.

Phlox spp.
Height and Spread vary
Who can resist sweetly scented phlox? *Phlox maculata* (height 3 ft/1 m, spread 18 in./45 cm) is the traditional phlox, with cylinders of small, fragrant, lavender-pink flowers from late spring to midsummer. *P. maculata* 'Omega' is white with a red eye, 'Alpha' is rose pink. The more common showy *P. paniculata* (height 4 ft/ 1.2 m, spread 2 ft/60 cm) has clusters of larger scented flowers later in the summer. *P. paniculata* 'White Admiral' is pure white and lightly scented; 'Graf Zeppelin' is white with a red eye. Phlox thrive in dappled shade in rich moist soil, and *P. paniculata* is prone to mildew and nematode attack, so propagate by root cuttings rather than division.

Polemonium caeruleum
JACOB'S LADDER
Height 2 ft/60 cm, Spread 2ft/60cm
So-called because the deep green leaflets are arranged at right angles one to another along the leaf ribs, Jacob's ladder has been a European country-garden staple since the 16th century. Open, bell-shaped, clear blue flowers with orange stamens cluster around the stems from late spring to midsummer, and the plant self-seeds freely in any soil in sun or partial shade. Look out for the white form, the lavender-flowered 'Lambrook Manor', and the deep blue 'Richardsonii'.

Polygonatum hybridum
SOLOMON'S SEAL
Height 3 ft/1 m, Spread 1 ft/30 cm
This ancient plant produces arching stems hung with drooping greenish white bells in late spring. They shine like pearls from shady places, and are ideal under shrubs or large summer-flowering perennials. Spread them by dividing the fleshy rhizomes.

Potentilla spp.
Height and Spread 18-24 in./45-60 cm
Herbaceous potentillas are useful long-flowering plants, thriving in sun or light shade in all but very heavy soils. They have strong-colored open-faced flowers in red, yellow, and orange from midsummer into fall and are good at the front of a bed where they can spread and sprawl contentedly. *P.* 'Gibson's Scarlet' is a fairly compact form with scarlet flowers from late spring. 'Yellow Queen' has semi-double bright yellow flowers. Some varieties self-seed; otherwise, spread them by division.

Primula spp.
PRIMROSE
Height and Spread vary
This huge family includes the first plants to flower in the garden to herald the spring, hence the name which means "first." Originally brought in from the wild, they have been in country gardens as long as there have been gardens. *Primula veris* is the native British cowslip (height and spread 9 in./20 cm) with spires of scented flowers. It prefers sun and a chalky alkaline soil and is wonderful in grass, but easiest to get going if you grow it in pots and plant out seedlings rather than sow seed direct. *P. vulgaris* (height and spread 6 in./ 15 cm) is the common primrose, happiest in semi-shade and moist soil. Among the many varieties 'Gigha' is pure white and 'Miss Indigo' is a maroonish-purple double form. *P. denticulata* (height 12-24 in./30-60 cm) is the drumstick primula with large, purple pompom flowers on tall stems. It also needs moist soil and is happy in sun or shade. *P. auricula* has groups of large, flat-faced flowers on short, stiff stems above evergreen waxy leaves. Show auriculas are not suitable for the flowerbed, but worth trying if you have a cool greenhouse: they are exquisite old-fashioned-looking flowers with lacy patterns and rich colors. Fragrant garden auriculas grow best in sun and moist but well-drained soil. One of the best is *P.* 'Old Yellow Dusty Miller' (height 6 in./15 cm, spread 10 in./25 cm) with yellow flowers with white floury eyes. *P. polyanthus,* a cross between primrose and cowslip that has produced sturdy plants with flowers in a huge range of colors, is just as easy

to grow as primroses. Candelabra primroses (height 20 in./50 cm spread 12 in./30 cm) have stiff stems bearing several bunches of flowers, evenly spaced down the stem, in late spring and early summer. They are ideal for the edge of a pond or a shady area because they need moist soil and some shade and don't mind getting wet. Look for *P. beesiana* with deep pinkish purple flowers. *P. pulverulenta* 'Bartley' has the palest pink flowers with red eyes.

Pulmonaria
LUNGWORT, SOLDIERS AND SAILORS
Height 12 in./30 cm, Spread 18 in./45 cm
Thought by 17th-century herbalists to resemble a lung with its large, silver-spotted and speckled leaves, pulmonaria is an excellent shade-loving plant, thriving under trees and shrubs and against cool north walls. In early spring clusters of pink, then violet-blue, tubular flowers appear before the leaves, which stay on the plant until late winter in some areas. Though they will flower in moist soil in sunny places, they are best in the shade where their spotted foliage will glimmer and shine. *P. officinalis* 'Sissinghurst White' has white flowers. *P. saccharata* 'Frühlingshimmel' has pale sky blue flowers with purple centers and particularly spotted leaves.

Ranunculus aconitifolius
BUTTERCUPS, FAIR MAIDS OF FRANCE
Height and Spread 3 ft/1 m
This lovely, non-invasive, cultivated buttercup used to be a great country garden favorite, bearing a froth of single, white, buttercup-style flowers in branching airy stems in late spring. Ranunculus thrive in damp places in sun or slight shade. They are trouble-free, spread happily, and are easy to propagate by division. Look for *R. aconitifolius* 'Flore Pleno', which has double white flowers.

Rudbeckia fulgida
CONEFLOWER
Height 2 ft/60 cm, Spread 12 in./30 cm
This very reliable, late summer-flowering daisy

has drooping yellow petals around a striking dark brown center. Happy in sun in almost any soil, it forms large clumps quickly and is easily divided to make new plants.

Salvia spp.
SAGE
Height and Spread vary
Salvia officinalis, common sage, would once have grown in every European country garden along with meadow clary *(S. pratensis)*, but there are dozens of good varieties among this enormous family of generally erect plants, which bear nettlelike flowers in spires above softly toothed or scalloped leaves. All are easy to grow but generally need shelter and warmth. Common favorites include the stunning *S. sclarea* var. *turkestanica* (height 3 ft/1 m, spread 18 in./45 cm) with its spires of pink-flecked white flowers all up its stem, *S. nemorosa* 'Ostfriesland' (height 3 ft/1 m, spread 24 in./60 cm) with deep blue-violet flowers from summer into fall, and the indispensable *S.* x *sylvestris* 'Mainacht' (height 24 in./60 cm, spread 18 in./45 cm), which has glorious, erect, indigo-blue flowers above a dense covering of small leaves. The mat-forming (height 6 in./15 cm, spread 12 in./30 cm) woolly, silver-leaved *S. caespitosa* has lovely lilac-pink flowers in summer, but it needs a very sheltered and free-draining spot to survive cold winters.

Saponaria officinalis
SOAPWORT
Height and Spread 3 ft/1 m
This plant with pretty, scented, pink, open flowers is a bit unkempt and best in larger gardens. It flowers from late summer until mid-fall, and self-seeds and spreads underground. Its slightly fleshy leaves produce a fine lather when crushed with a little water, and are still used by conservators to clean precious textiles.

Scabiosa caucasica
SCABIOUS
Height and Spread 2 ft/60 cm

Originally a common British wildflower, cultivated forms of this pretty pincushion-headed flower come not only in traditional blue with a ring of white petals, but also in white and lavender. Plant scabious freely in dry, sunny spots around the beds, where their long stems and shaggy heads make them very easy companions for most other plants. Divide plants every couple of years to keep them flowering at their best.

Sedum spectabile
ICE PLANT, LIGHTNING PLANT
Height and Spread 18 in./45 cm
Sedums have distinctive thick fleshy stems and leaves, and flat heads of tiny starry flowers in summer and fall. They will grow in any dry sunny spot and are excellent value for their structural shape, long-lasting fleshy foliage, and their flat heads that are adored by bees, butterflies, and insects. Perhaps not the most exciting plants on their own, they seem to complement any neighboring plants and should definitely be included near the front of a bed, if only for their fall color.

Sisyrinchium spp.
Height and Spread vary
Sisyrinchium striatum is an erect plant (height 3 ft/90 cm, spread 10 in./25 cm) with stiff, grayish green, sword-shaped leaves and spires of clustered, pale yellow flowers in midsummer. It provides a useful vertical plant in a sunny bed and will also grow in gravel or paving. 'Aunt May' is a lovely white form. Although *Sisyrinchium californicum* is only half-hardy, these lovely miniature irislike plants (6 in./15 cm tall) with sword-shaped leaves self-seed freely in dry, sunny ground and along the edges of paths, bearing star-shaped flowers that are either dark-veined bright yellow or bright blue.

Stachys lanata
LAMB'S EARS
Height 18 in./45 cm, Spread 12 in./30 cm
Another must-have for any self-respecting country garden, Lamb's Ears make a lovely felty

carpet of woolly leaves. Deep pink flowers are produced in summer, but it is the foliage that is special, perfect at the front of a sunny bed and also particularly fine between slim-stemmed plants and under roses. It doesn't like wet soil, but spreads freely in dry conditions and can be divided often. *S. lanata* 'Byzantina' has large leaves; 'Silver Carpet' is a non-flowering form that produces a low carpet of leaves.

Thalictrum aquilegifolium
MEADOW RUE
Height 3 ft/1m, Spread 24 in./60cm
This stately upright plant has delicate foliage similar to aquilegias and clusters of fluffy flowers in blues to pinkish purple, and there's a good white form. It likes sun and moisture-retentive soil, and is perfect toward the back of a bed where its flowers float like clouds above the fine foliage. *Thalictrum delavayi* has numerous long-stalked fluffy lilac flowers.

Verbascum spp.
MULLEIN
Height 3-4 ft/1-1.2 m, Spread 18 in./45 cm

All mulleins are happy in sun and dry soil. *Verbascum chaixii* has small yellow flowers with a purple center; *V. chaixii album* is the attractive white form. They seed prolifically all around the garden, and are as contented in paths as in beds. The purple mullein *(V. phoeniceum)* flowers in a range of pastel shades and also seeds generously. There are many attractive hybrids, such as the popular light brown *V.* 'Helen Johnson', but they are much less sturdy and tend to be rather short-lived plants.

Verbena bonariensis
Height 6 ft/2 m, Spread 18 in./45 cm
Verbena is a stiff and upright plant, forming very airy clumps topped with clusters of bright flowers on long stalks with insignificant, thin, lance-shaped leaves. It is another useful see-through plant that can be placed anywhere in the flowerbed from front to back, and it will grow as happily in thin, poor, dry soil as in richer beds. *V. hastata* is a slightly less common form with stiffer panicles of violet-blue to pinkish flowers.

Veronica spicata
Height and Spread 15-24 in./40-60 cm
Veronica is a favorite for its intense blue flowers and delicate habit. A mat of fine-toothed leaves supports straight flowering stems with pyramids of star-shaped flowers. Easy to grow in sun and dry soil, it is one of the best blues for an early summer bed. *V. spicata* 'Saraband' has violet-blue flowers over hairy silvery foliage. *V. spicata* 'Heidekind' is compact with raspberry-pink flowers and silver-gray leaves.

Viola spp.
VIOLET, VIOLA, PANSY
Height and Spread vary
The scented sweet violet *(V. odorata)* (height and spread 6 in./15 cm) flowers in spring and should be allowed to spread under the shade of larger plants in your beds, as they've been doing in gardens for about a thousand years. *V. tricolor* is the original "heart's ease" with its face of yellow, purple, blue, and cream and flowers all summer. *V. wittrockiana* is the large-flowered garden pansy, with hundreds of varieties in dozens of colors.

Sisyrinchium striatum

Thalictrum delavayi

Viola 'Jackanapes' (named after Gertrude Jekyll's pet monkey)

Ornamental grasses

Ornamental grasses are comparative newcomers to our beds, but they are good candidates for country gardens. They are easy to look after and provide a long season of interest with their flexible leaves, delicate flowerheads, good fall colors, and striking seedheads. There are forms to suit most situations: some arch upward, others stick close to the ground; some form neat clumps, others spread to form wide carpets. This huge diversity means there will be something suitable for every type of garden and situation. There are low grasses for the fronts of beds and towering subjects for the back. Tough upright species can provide structure and support to lower-growing floppy plants, and the upright habit of many grasses complements tall spiky verbascums or aconites or contrasts with flat-topped flowers such as achilleas. They are also ideal companions for large-leaved plants, and their many different colors suggest interesting color associations.

Although most are deciduous perennials, grasses such as *Calamagrostis* provide interest over a very long period, from the moment their fresh spring growth appears to the time you cut down their winter skeletons to make way for new growth. Consequently, they can provide a good framework for a bed where other plants will flower and decline within a much shorter period. The autumnal colors of *Panicum* varieties are very striking, and others produce particularly attractive seedheads that stand well into winter. And of course grasses are among the least static of all garden plants: tall varieties will whisper in the slightest breath of air, and even short tidy clumps can suddenly throw up tall, elegant flowerheads to provide a whole new feeling to the space and plantings around them.

Miscanthus sinensis 'Morning light' is stunning at the back of a large border or on its own as a point of interest in a larger garden. Its stiff stems and generous feathery seedheads make striking features in any winter landscape.

Calamagrostis x acutiflora 'Karl Foerster'

FEATHERED REED GRASS

Height 6 ft/1.75 m, Spread 20 in./50 cm.

Will grow in sun in any soil. The earliest perennial grass, it shoots into growth in very early spring. Flower stems rise in early summer and develop narrow ears the color of wheat that stand at attention well into winter. Excellent with asters, rudbeckias, and veronicas. *C x acutiflora* 'Stricta' is slightly taller with red-brown ears.

Carex elata 'Aurea'

BOWLES GOLDEN SEDGE

Height and Spread 20 in./50 cm.

Likes moist conditions and partial shade. Evergreen, clump-forming perennial with golden yellow leaves; provides good winter and spring color; excellent against bronze foliage or deep purple tulips.

Festuca glauca

BLUE FESCUE GRASS

Height 12 in./30 cm, Spread 9 in./20 cm

This grass requires well-drained soil and a sunny position, and won't tolerate wet feet. It forms dense mounds of blue-green leaves with small, open flowerheads in summer. The color is best on thin, dry soils. 'Azurit' is a more upright form with particularly blue foliage. 'Elijah Blue' is the most searingly blue of all. 'Silbersee' is a very small, compact variety with silver-blue leaves.

Miscanthus

Height and Spread vary

Members of this important group of trouble-free ornamental grasses are very adaptable and remain features in the winter landscape, their stiff stems and fingerlike flowerheads resisting the weather. Growing in any soil in full sun, they take two or three years to become established and spread vigorously but can be easily contained by regular division. *Miscanthus sinensis* 'Gracillimus' or maiden grass (height 6 ft/1.75 m, spread 5 ft/1.5 m) produces very narrow arching leaves in dense compact clumps, but shows its white feathery flowers reluctantly in early fall in cool northern climates. 'Graziella' has a similar habit but readily produces large silver-white plumes that stand out high above its foliage. Flowering is also unreliable in northern areas for *M.* var. *purpurascens*, but grow this particular grass for its foliage color. A purplish wash develops over summer, intensifying to a rich reddish brown in the fall.

Molinia caerulea

PURPLE MOOR GRASS

Height 3 ft/90 cm, Spread 12 in./30 cm

This grass grows in the wild on acid and mineral-deficient soils, but is happy in any average garden soil in sun or semi-shade. Typically, long straight flower stems rise well clear of the neat clumps of broad grayish green leaves in late summer. This grass is excellent for a fairly forward position in a bed since you can virtually see through its delicate, purple, spiky flowerheads, which don't obscure other lower plants. Rain may make plants bow their heads to the ground but they soon recover as they dry out.

Stipa gigantea

GOLDEN OATS

Height 7 ft/2.25 m, Spread 3 ft/1 m.

If you can, make space in well-drained soil in a sunny position for this stunning grass. Spectacular flowerheads rise from moderate-sized, dense evergreen clumps of gray-green leaves, which provide a good contrast to more solid evergreen shapes. Even in winter the dead flowerheads add color as they change from parchment shades to rusty brown when wet. Full of movement, stipas rustle satisfactorily in the wind. *Stipa arundinacea*, pheasant grass, will sit happily in heavier soil. It is grown largely for the color of its loose clumps of shiny leaves that develop into rich orange-red, topped with purplish green flower spikes in the fall. The color is particularly striking in winter.

Carex elata 'Aurea'

Festuca glauca 'Elijah blue'

Molinia caerulea

Annuals

Annuals have been the cinderellas of flowering plants for far too long, often dismissed by those that favor perennials. But these dismissive gardeners are missing out, because annuals give great flexibility, providing instant bursts of color and filling spaces. They're especially useful in smaller gardens — planted in groups among early-flowering perennials to introduce more flowers as the perennials struggle and fade, or while later perennials wait to grow into their full charms. And they're wonderful to complement more permanent color schemes and carry them through the seasons.

They are also often slandered for their bright, unsubtle colors, but their brilliant hues can be perfect in country gardens. Another great bonus is the way many annuals self-seed to reappear where they feel like it, year after year. This is an important part of the charm of any country garden, and you can always pull them up if they appear where you don't want them.

Hardy annuals are the easiest of all to sow. Just scratch a line in the soil and sow them as soon as the soil has warmed up in early spring. Some can be sown again in early summer for continuous displays, but remember to thin them out to the required distance when they have a few leaves showing. Don't be tempted to leave great clumps of seedlings because they will crowd each other out, and plants that are too closely spaced will be poor, stunted things, blossoming only for a stressed short period.

Half-hardy annuals must be sown in pots or trays under cover and planted out only when all danger of frost has passed.

Annuals are easy to grow, not much bothered by climate. Unless specifically stated, all those listed prefer a sunny position and light fertile soil, but most will tolerate a bit of shade and most weather conditions except for persistent wetness.

Don't shy away from using annuals to keep borders bright all summer long, including clumps of cosmos, dahlias, marigolds, salvias, sweet peas, and sunflowers.

SAVING SEED

■ All country gardeners used to save and sow their own seed, or share it with friends and neighbors. All annuals, most biennials, and some perennials can be increased this way.

■ When plants have finished flowering, allow their seedheads to ripen and collect them just before the casings split open and seeds fall to the ground. You must collect seeds from dry plants.

■ If you worry about timing or the weather is damp, pull up whole plants and hang them to dry in an airy place with a paper bag over their heads to catch seed as it drops.

■ You may need to separate the seeds from their casings, either picking through them by hand or shaking them in a flat basket or sifter.

■ Save clean seed in well-labeled paper envelopes in a cool dry place. Sow seed from annuals in spring, that from biennials and perennials in fall.

■ Some of the easiest seeds to save are beans, bachelor's buttons, peas, hollyhocks, foxgloves, marigolds, nasturtiums, morning glory, and sweet peas, but sweet pea seeds must be sown the following spring since they don't keep more than one season.

TOP TEN SELF-SEEDERS

Alcea rosea
'Chater's Double' has large double flowers in bright and dark shades.

Aquilegia vulgaris
These self-seed freely.

Digitalis purpurea
Common foxgloves are variable, with purple, pink, or white flowers.

Limnanthes douglasii
Low-growing, unstoppable, and attractive to aphid-munching insects.

Lunaria annua
Purple flowers are followed by silver "moon penny" seedheads.

Nigella damascena
This grows in every nook and cranny.

Oenothera biennis
Allow these to self-seed freely and enjoy their evening scent and late summer flowers.

Papaver somniferum
Peony-flowered varieties have large double frilly flowers in shades of pink.

Polemonium caeruleum
The white variety self-seeds less prolifically, but gets there in the end.

Verbena bonariensis
This rampant self-seeder is a valuable "see-through" plant.

Ageratum houstonianum
Height 8 in./20 cm
This hummock-forming, hardy annual has clusters of attractive fluffy flowers, traditionally blue as in 'Blue Horizon', but there is a good rose pink form, 'Bavaria'. If you deadhead fairly rigorously, it will flower in a sunny position throughout the summer and well into the fall.

Agrostemma githago
CORNCOCKLE
Height 2-4 ft/60 cm-1.2 m
Once a common wildflower considered a pestilential weed of European wheatfields, corncockle's delicate, open-faced pink flowers appear above tall spindly stems and narrow, grayish green leaves, and float happily around more substantial plantings in any bed, or mixed with other annuals. Like most other flowers that have been brought in from the wild, it thrives just as well on fairly impoverished soil as in fertile beds. *A. githago* 'Milas' has tall pink blooms with paler centers. *A. githago* 'Ocean Pearl' is also tall with pure white petals with a fine black speckle. 'Purple Queen' is shorter (2-3 ft/60-90 cm) with rich purplish blossoms.

Amaranthus caudatus
LOVE LIES BLEEDING/PRINCE'S FEATHER
Height 5 ft/1.5 m
This splendid, showy, half-hardy annual has bright green foliage and magnificent crimson-tasseled flowers. Although noted in British country gardens in the 17th century, it has always found more favor in its native North America where many good varieties are widely available.

Anchusa capensis
Height 7 in./18 cm
Often grown as a biennial, the beautiful white-throated, blue starry flowers of this erect Mediterranean wildflower makes it a great addition to any garden. 'Blue Angel' is a neat upright variety with ultramarine flowers, and the taller 'Blue Bird' (18 in./45 cm) proffers indigo-blue blooms.

Antirrhinum spp.
SNAPDRAGON
Height 6 in.–2 ft/15-50 cm
Technically perennials but grown as annuals, snapdragons are old country-garden favorites,

Clarkia elegans

Consolida ajacis

available in a range of colors and heights. Tall forms can be grown for cutting or for filling gaps in a perennial bed, shorter ones for bedding. It's best to sow them in trays or pots and plant out, after frost has passed, into rich, well-drained soil. Keep them well watered and regularly picked to encourage long flowering. 'Black Prince' (18 in./45 cm) has dark crimson flowers and deep greenish red leaves. 'White Wonder' (8 in./20 cm) has large white flowers, but there are dozens to choose from.

Calendula officinalis
POT MARIGOLD
Height 12-24 in./30-60 cm
This typical country-garden plant used to be widely grown in pots, flowerbeds, and herb gardens. There are lots of good cultivars with daisylike single or double flowers in shades of orange, yellow, and cream, many with darker disk flowerets in the center. They flower profusely all summer long and well into the fall.

Centaurea cyanus
BACHELOR'S BUTTONS, CORNFLOWER
Height 30 in./75 cm
The traditional bright blue flower, once a staple wheatfield weed, perks up summer and fall beds if you sow seed early and late. They are called bachelor's buttons, apparently because their shaggy heads resembled the bits of cloth that farmworkers, most of them unmarried, used as buttons in the 18th and 19th centuries. An old name, hurtsickles, originated because their tough stems could blunt a sickle. Bachelor's buttons germinate readily and grow fast, so they are perfect plants for impatient children of all ages; and the deep purple, almost black variety 'Black Ball' is irresistible among brighter summer flowers and roses.

Cerinthe major 'Purpurascens'
Height 24 in./60 cm
Definitely not a traditional country-garden plant, cerinthe is one of those plants that has taken gardens by storm in the last decade. Generous, fleshy, blue-green, cabbagelike leaves with a lax droopy habit produce bracts of almost navy blue flowers all summer. Cerinthe is a bushy plant, best grown in generous clumps, a perfect companion to shrubby lavender and more disciplined plants with fine foliage. Although it thrives in full sun, it will also tolerate partial shade.

Clarkia
CLARKIA, GODETIA
Height 12-18 in./30-45 cm
Long a country favorite, its spreading funnel-shaped flowers are pink, lavender, purple, and white. They are worth growing for cutting, and they are among the few useful annuals that grow happily in partial shade.

Convolvulus tricolor
Height 12 in./30 cm
This sprawling or climbing annual suffers from guilt by association with the pestilential (but beautiful) bindweed, but it is a bright and useful plant with large blue flowers with a white throat and yellow eye. Being annual, at the end of summer it dies and quietly disappears, quite unlike bindweed.

Consolida spp.
LARKSPUR
Height 4 ft/1.2 m
Also known as annual delphiniums, larkspur produces beautiful spikes of predominantly violet, blue, pink, and white blooms on upright stems. Plants are very fast growing, indispensable for filling late summer gaps in your beds, and good for cutting. 'Kingsize Scarlet' is a 4-foot (1.2 m) variety with spires of scarlet. Another similarly tall variety, 'Earl Grey', has curious slate-gray double flowers.

Coreopsis grandiflora
Height 12-24 in./30-60 cm, Spread 18 in./45 cm
Technically perennial but grown as an annual. Broad, single, golden yellow daisylike flowers with darker centers are produced from late spring through to late summer. 'Early Sunrise' is a good deep yellow semi-double variety (18 in./45 cm). The compact 'Gold Star' (12 in./30 cm) has golden flowerheads with rolled petals.

Cosmos spp.
MEXICAN ASTER
Height 3 ft/1 m
These tall, bushy annuals have ferny foliage topped by fragile saucer-shaped flowers from midsummer well into the fall. The most common cosmos are red, pink, and white. They are among the easiest annuals to thread through perennial beds. The popular purplish-brown Cosmos atrosanguineus 'Chocolate' is an unusual and useful chocolate-scented form, perfect for continuing a deep jeweled color theme into the fall. Another favorite is the crinkled white C. bipinnatus 'Purity'.

Dahlia spp.
Height 18 in.-5 ft/45 cm-1.5 m
Largely ignored by serious gardeners for decades, dahlias are wonderful country-garden plants, providing a bright injection of color to a late summer garden. Not strictly annuals, but tender perennials, all dahlia tubers are frost tender. They should be lifted in the fall and replanted after the last frosts in spring, or grow them as annuals and plant fresh tubers each year. They like well-drained, rich soil and a sunny spot. Enjoy rifling through the pages of a specialist nursery's catalog — there are hundreds of dahlias to choose from, with single flowers, doubles, pompoms, shaggy heads, and peony faces, in a wide range of colors. Two favorites to brighten the back of a bed from midsummer to the first frosts are 'Arabian Knight' (height 5 ft/1.5 m) with glorious medium green foliage and brilliant red flowers, and the stunning bright red 'Bishop of Llandaff' (height 3 ft/1 m) with superb bronze foliage. 'White Alva's' has giant white flowers, but you'll soon find your own favorites. The only thing to watch out for is virus resistance — ask your supplier, since some exhibition varieties are very susceptible and shouldn't be included in a country garden.

Eschscholzia spp.
CALIFORNIA POPPY
Height 12 in./30 cm
This is an invaluable addition to any flowerbed. Allow the red, white, pink, and orange flowers to weave through your perennials in late spring and summer, or grow them in gravel where you'll see their fine blue-green foliage as well as the silky paper-thin flowers.

Gypsophila spp.
BABY'S BREATH
Height 18 in./45 cm
Clouds of daintiest white or slightly pink veined flowers are produced over delicate but stiff-stemmed foliage in mid- and late summer, excellent for cutting.

Helianthus spp.
SUNFLOWER
Height 6-10 ft/2-3 m
No one could call sunflowers beautiful, but they are charming and great fun to grow, though some think their best use is in the bird feeder and the compost heap! They do make an attractive summer screen at one end of a vegetable patch. There are some interesting variations on the generally yellow color: 'Velvet Queen' has coppery red flowers; 'Russian Black' has huge deep brown flowers; 'Italian White' has cream and gold flowers with an almost black center.

Helichrysum bracteatum syn. *Bracteantha bracteata*
EVERLASTING FLOWER, STRAWFLOWER
Height 12 in.-4 ft/30 cm-1.2 m
From late spring to fall, erect wiry stems bear strawlike, bright white, pink, red, or yellow flowers. They're good gap fillers for a sunny, well-drained bed and make attractive cut and dried flowers.

Heliotropium arborescens
HELIOTROPE
Height 15 in./40 cm
Incredibly popular in country gardens for centuries, this half-hardy annual forms compact, fragrant cushions of deep purple flowers, but it's best to take cuttings and overwinter them in a frost-free place because plants grown from seed rarely have the fragrance that should be their hallmark. Extremely tender, heliotrope should be the last plant out in spring.

Iberis umbellata
CANDYTUFT
Height 8 in./20 cm
It's hard to imagine an old-fashioned country garden without cheerful mounds of candytuft appearing to edge a bed or path somewhere in summer. This is another ideal child's plant — seeds germinate in a flash, flower quickly, and fade away fast, before interest is lost. White, lavender, pink, and red forms exist.

Lathyrus odoratus
SWEET PEA
Height varies
No garden should be without the inviting cheerful colors and heady fragrance of sweet peas in summer. Choose old-fashioned varieties such as the two-toned purple and violet 'Matucana' or 'Cupani's Original' for the most evocative heady scent. Fortunately, breeders do seem to be recognizing that scent is the whole point of sweet peas for so many of us, and it is reappearing in many seed mixtures marketed as "old-fashioned." Soak sweet pea seeds in water overnight before sowing in pots under cover (on windowsills is fine) in early spring; they'll shoot away almost as soon as they touch the potting medium, or sow them later straight into the soil. Keep picking sweet peas to prolong their flowering period, and plant them in full sun in moisture-retentive soil. They look great climbing up supports in pots by a front door and are traditionally grown on wigwams in the vegetable garden.

Lavatera trimestris
ANNUAL MALLOW
Height 2-4 ft/60 cm-1.2 m
Many gardeners appreciate this easy-to-grow, branching plant with large mallowlike flowers in pink and white.

Helianthus annuus

Lathyrus odoratus

Limnanthes douglasii

DOUGLAS' MEADOW FOAM, POACHED
EGG PLANT

Height 6 in./15 cm

The yellow-centered, white-edged meadow foam should be in every garden. Not only sunny and cheerful, it is also one of the best plants to attract many of the predatory insects that munch the aphids in your garden. Another bonus is its freewheeling self-seeding habit; it springs up each year without fail to form mounds here and there. Plants are easy to uproot if you don't want them growing where they have seeded.

Limonium sinuatum

SEA LAVENDER, STATICE

Height 16 in./40 cm

These old-fashioned annuals seem to have lost popularity in the last few decades, but they are very attractive, upright splashes of color, excellent for cutting and drying. Erect stems are laden with clusters of tiny funnel-shaped, pink, white, or blue flowers that are easy to dry if you pick them when fully open. The taller 'Forever Gold' (24 in./60 cm) has larger, tightly packed flowers in bright yellow.

Lunaria annua

HONESTY, MONEY PLANT

Height 3 ft/90 cm

Strong branching stems with spikes of pretty purple or white flowers are followed by attractive transparent "moon penny" seedheads much liked by children. Honesty thrives in shade and almost any soil conditions, self-seeding without fail year after year.

Matthiola incana

BROMPTON STOCK

Height 18 in./45 cm

Biennials but treated as annuals, these early summer flowering blossoms are grown for their delicious old-fashioned clove scent that gets noticeably stronger at night. There are single and double forms in pink, crimson, lavender, and mauve. *Matthiola incana* var. *annua* is the true annual stock, also known as ten-week stock. It is traditionally used in summer bedding displays but is at home anywhere in a flowerbed.

Nicotiana sylvestris

TOBACCO PLANT

Height 5 ft/1.2 m

There's nothing quite like the scent of tobacco plants on late summer evenings, so do try to remember to sow them each year. Avoid at all costs the tobacco plants sold as front-of-bed plants in garden centers; they have had the scent and style bred out of them. *N. sylvestris* produces great sprays of heavily scented tubular white flowers above generous shining green leaves. It almost seems to glow at dusk, attracting night-flying pollinators into your yard. Easy to grow from seed sown indoors in spring, it thrives in any well-drained soil and sunny spot, flowering happily in all but persistently wet summers. *N. langsdorffi* is a neater (height 3 ft/90 cm) form with smaller leaves and delicate greenish flowers, better for smaller gardens or troughs.

Nigella damascena

LOVE-IN-A-MIST

Height 18 in./45cm

Love-in-a-mist is justly well-loved, with its frilly foliage and feathery round whiskered flowers that bloom throughout the summer, followed by striking horned seedpods that split to spread their seed freely. In addition to blue, there are pink and white forms, but many stick with the pale blue 'Miss Jekyll', which looks wonderful springing up wherever it can find a space, complementing everything it comes against. 'Oxford Blue' is a double dark blue form with dark seedpods. It is such a delicate plant that it never seems to take over; even when it spreads everywhere, stronger plants will push it out of the way, or it is easily removed. Love-in-a-mist's only disadvantage is that you can't transplant the fragile seedlings.

Papaver spp.

POPPY

Height 1-3 ft/30-90 cm

Perfect for spontaneous bursts of color, there's little more cheering than a profusion of

Lunaria annua

Nicotiana sylvestris (foreground)

poppies. The blue-green leaves and stems of opium poppies *(P. somniferum)* are bright contrasts to darker green foliage, their sumptuous pink- and raspberry-colored heads of papery petals and dark centers inviting a second look. Each bloom lasts only a few days, but each seedpod that follows contains enough seeds to cover your garden the following year, and for years to come. Leave them to romp among your vegetables as well as in your flowerbeds. Field poppies *(P. rhoeas)* are also happy additions to a garden, bright flecks of color for a single day above fine whiskery foliage, and you can find excellent selections of the pale, ruffle-edged but bright-flowered Shirley poppies. The gaudy colors of Iceland poppies *(P. nudicaule)* are also welcome additions. It's easy to scatter poppy seeds in spring, or if you remember, scatter ripe seed in the fall for an earlier display.

Phacelia tanacetifolia
FIDDLENECK
Height 6-12 in./15-30 cm

Tropaeolum majus

Everyone should grow this scented, deep blue-flowered annual, if only because it is a favorite for bees and other insects. Good at the front of a bed, it can also be used as green manure in the vegetable bed, adding fertility while buzzing with insects all summer, and looking delightful.

Reseda odorata
MIGNONETTE
Height 12 in./30 cm

Not the most stunning plant to look at, mignonette has insignificant greenish white flowers and sprawls in an unkempt way over the edge of a bed. However, it's worth growing a patch of mignonette for its incredible strong fragrance. It was very fashionable in the 18th and 19th centuries, when no garden in town or country was without it, and it was most popular for windowboxes and containers.

Salvia spp.
SAGE
Height varies

There are numerous annual salvias, but there

Salvia farinacea 'Victoria'

are more interesting tender varieties of perennial salvias that have to be grown as annuals. *Salvia patens* (height and spread 18-24 in./45-60 cm) has pairs of vivid gentian-blue flowers above typical soft green salvia foliage. *S. patens* 'Cambridge Blue' has paler blue blooms. *S. farinacea* (height 24 in./60 cm, spread 12 in./30 cm) has white mealy stems with dense spikes of deep lavender flowers produced from summer to fall.

Tropaeolum majus
NASTURTIUM
Height varies

Another typical country-garden plant. Its brilliant red, orange, and yellow trumpet-shaped flowers are often seen clustering on paths, sprawling over walls and banks, or scrambling out of pots. Nasturtiums give their best show in really poor soil, so they are great for summer color when you're starting a garden and haven't yet had time to improve the soil, or for brightening a dull spot where nothing else will thrive, but they also put on a good show in fertile soil. As a bonus, every part of the plant is edible, and the leaves and flowers are great additions to summer salads. There are nasturtiums for every situation, from neat clump-forming varieties to prolific climbing and trailing forms. All are cheerful, easy to grow, and likely to self-seed. Breeders have improved nasturtium flowers to create semi-double and even double blooms, with or without the typical "spurs" of the species.

Zinnia
Height 24-30 in./60-75 cm

This huge family of plants has generous daisylike flowers in a showy range of colors, particularly worth growing as cut flowers because they last in water for up to two weeks. Sown under cover in spring and planted out into a very warm spot in full sun and fertile soil, they will flower from midsummer until frost. 'Envy' has double lime green petals and a slightly darker center. 'Red Spider' has spidery scarlet petals with a deep maroon center.

Zinnia

TEN FAVORITE ANNUALS FOR POTS AND BASKETS

Bidens ferulifolia
Height 12 in./30 cm. Irresistible, delicate, golden yellow daisy with fernlike leaves, particularly good paired with trailing ivy.

Cerinthe minor aurea
Height 15-18 in./40 cm. Glitzy dwarf variety of *Cerinthe major* with green and gold flowers amid white spotted foliage.

Cosmos atrosanguineum
Height 15 in./40 cm. Actually a perennial, but treated as an annual in cool climates, the deep maroon single flowers of chocolate cosmos are best appreciated in pots where the scent can be inhaled.

Felicia
Height 10 in./25 cm. Blue daisy flowers with yellow centers and feathery foliage, this flowers from early summer until frost. Low-growing *F. heterophylla* has pale blue flowers over gray foliage.

Heliotropium
Height 15 in./40 cm. Consider this highly fragrant, sunny favorite for tubs and windowboxes.

Matthiolia incana 'Cinderella' series
Height 8-10 in./20-25 cm. Lovely in containers, these highly scented stocks bloom in shades of crimson and lilac.

Nicotiana sylvestris
Height 5 ft/1.2 m. Nothing beats stately, highly scented tobacco plants for tubs by the door. Don't be tempted by compact forms without scent.

Pelargonium spp.
Height 6-24 in./15-60 cm. Pelargoniums thrive in sun all summer if deadheaded regularly and well fed and watered. Choose trailing forms with lemon- or camphor-scented foliage, green or cream ivy-shaped or rounded blotched leaves, and single or double flowers in white and shades of pink, red, and lavender.

Petunia spp.
Height 12-24 in./30-60 cm. Don't resist cheerful petunias with their unsubtle colors and open trumpet faces. Look for old-fashioned, highly scented *P. integrifolia* — masses of magenta flowers that droop over a basket or pot.

Ornamental cabbage
Height 9 in./22 cm. Plant fall containers with deep purple, green, and cream cabbages with frilled edges.

Climbers

Use climbers to cover as many vertical surfaces as possible in a country garden. Grow them over arches and arbors, and train them to clamber up freestanding wooden frames and wicker pyramids to add height to your beds. Covering the walls and fences of a small yard makes the space feel larger as well as more interesting, and the straightest boundaries lose their oppressive starkness when they are dripping with foliage and flowers.

Most climbers like rich, moisture-retentive ground, so prepare generous planting holes very well, particularly as the soil beside a building is always impoverished and dry. Take particular care about watering climbers, especially in their early years, and never plant closer than 15 inches (40 cm) from a house wall. Make sure you can get at plants easily to tie them in or prune them when necessary, and train climbers on wires or trellis at least 1.5 inches (4 cm) away from the walls. This gives them more room to climb securely and provides useful space for wildlife to shelter. The other thing to watch is vigor — an enthusiastic clematis such as *C. montana* will satisfactorily cover a fence in a couple of years from a standing start. However, it will keep on going at the same speed for years and can smother everything else in a small yard, or cause problems with your neighbors. Other perennial climbers, such as tulip magnolia *(Magnolia × soulangeana)* grow more slowly. If you really need instant summer cover, try annual climbers while you get perennials established.

Right: Lonicera pericylemenum 'Serotina' is a perfect plant to clamber over a pergola, spreading its heady scent in midsummer.

Far right: This wooden arch is covered in late spring and early summer with a mass of Clematis montana 'grandiflora alba' and Rosa 'Sombreuil'.

FAVORITE CLEMATIS FOR ARCHES

Clematis armandii is a tender evergreen.

Clematis cirrhosa is another evergreen that flowers in late winter.

Clematis durandii produces glorious dark violet flowers with yellow stamens in summer.

Clematis flammula produces starry white flowers in late summer and early fall; it needs a sheltered aspect in full sun with roots in deep shade.

Clematis florida produces creamy green-striped flowers with purple centers in midsummer. Plant it in a sheltered place in full sun with the roots well shaded.

Clematis 'Jackmanii' flowers late with huge dark purple blooms.

Clematis macropetala is an old favorite with bell-shaped flowers.

Clematis montana is a free-flowering, vigorous grower.

Clematis rehderiana is a vigorous spreading climber with downy leaves and bell-shaped, fragrant, pale yellow flowers in late summer to mid-fall.

Clematis tangutica has unusual yellow flowers produced well into fall.

Clematis viticella is the oldest garden clematis.

Akebia quinata

CHOCOLATE VINE

Height 20 ft/6 m

This exotic-looking, semi-evergreen plant has attractive rounded leaves and chocolate-scented, pinkish purple flowers in early spring, followed by violet-gray pendulous fruit in fall. Hardier than its appearance suggests, it will thrive in most soils on a sunny and sheltered wall where its early flowers won't be spoiled by late frost.

Campsis spp.

TRUMPET VINE

Height 20-30 ft/6-9 m

This small-leaved, vigorous climber needs a sunny sheltered site where it will thrive to produce striking clusters of trumpet-shaped flowers among its dark green leaves in the early fall. *Campsis radicans,* the common trumpet creeper, is the hardiest, with red and gold flowers. *C. grandiflora* has the most spectacular orange to red flowers, but is the least hardy.

Ceanothus spp.

CALIFORNIAN LILAC

Height and Spread vary

If blue is a favorite color, and your yard isn't exposed, you must have ceanothus. Among the many varieties of this attractive shrub are some excellent evergreen climbers, most with small, serrated, shiny dark green leaves and panicles of flowers from spring onward in all shades of blue. *C.* 'Concha' (height and spread 3 m/10 ft) has tiny dark green leaves and a profusion of purplish red buds that open into large clusters of purplish blue flowers in late spring, so many that the whole bush seems to turn blue. Although severe frost will scorch branches and buds, this variety recovers well. Vigorous, wide-spreading *C. arboreus* 'Trewithen Blue' (height and spread 20 ft/6 m) has scented mid-blue flowers in spring and early summer; *C.* 'Autumnal Blue' (height and spread 3 m/ 10 ft) produces generous panicles of sky-blue flowers in late summer and fall. The drawbacks with ceanothus are that plants are not long lived and sometimes suddenly die for no apparent reason, and some are very frost-tender.

Chaenomeles japonica

ORNAMENTAL QUINCE

Height 6 ft/2 m

This very hardy, flowering wall shrub was a Victorian cottage-garden favorite. It produces bright orange flowers in spring, followed by yellow applelike fruits in the fall that stay on the bushes until after Christmas in some areas. Plant against a fence or wall and tie it firmly; then trim to shape when you feel the urge. *C. speciosa* 'Nivalis' has pure white flowers, and *C. speciosa* 'Moerloosei' (also known as 'Apple Blossom') has white flowers tinged with pink.

Clematis spp.

CLEMATIS

Height and Spread vary

The clematis family is incredibly diverse. Flowers range from 1-20 inches (2-25 cm) across, and varieties can clamber rampantly or stay neat and low growing, so there is something for every situation. In general, the small-flowered varieties are more vigorous than the larger-flowered ones, so choose carefully according to your space. Clematis need shaded roots, so if you plant in full sun it's best to plant something else at the clematis's base. Although all other container-grown plants should be planted at the level

Campsis radicans

Clematis 'President'

Clematis tangutica

they grow in the pot, plant clematis slightly lower, so that it will regenerate if attacked by wilt, the most common clematis disease, which withers shoots above ground.

Pruning is a question that confuses gardeners, but it is not complicated. If the clematis flowers before midsummer, prune it after flowering by cutting side shoots back to within a bud or two of the main branches, or just clip it to keep it under control; if it flowers later in the summer, cut it back to within 6 inches (15 cm) of the ground in late winter. *C. montana* varieties are very vigorous and will swiftly cover a building or trawl along a wall, but if you have space, do include it for its profusion of small white slightly almond-scented flowers in early summer. *C. montana* 'Elizabeth' is a pink form. *C. alpina* (6-10 ft/2-3 m) is a compact variety perfect for small yards, with masses of dainty, blue, bell-shaped flowers with a white central tuft in early summer, followed by fluffy seedheads, and it usually flowers a second time in late summer. *C. macropetala* (6-10 ft/2-3 m) is another old favorite, flowering in spring and early summer with masses of dark blue or violet semi-double

Cobaea scandens

bell-shaped flowers, with cream inner petals followed by long-lasting, silvery seedheads. *C. tangutica* (15-20 ft/5-6 m) has abundant, solitary, bell-shaped yellow flowers from midsummer to late fall. *C. armandii* (10-15 ft/3-5 m) bears gloriously scented white flowers in late winter over glossy evergreen leaves, but is very wind-sensitive and needs shelter. *C. cirrhosa* (8-10 ft/2-3 m) is an evergreen variety that flowers in late winter. Its creamy-green, open bell-shaped flowers are softly speckled with red. 'Balearica' has more strongly speckled fragrant flowers, but is slightly tender. *C. viticella* (6-12 ft/2-4 m) is the oldest garden variety, with small reddish violet, blue, or white flowers. It flowers from midsummer to early fall and is ideal for growing through other spent climbers or up an obelisk to give a late lift to a bed. *C.* 'Perle d'Azur' (10 ft/3m) is a late free-flowering climber with masses of azure blue flowers with creamy green centers. Among the dozens of large-flowered clematis, favorite cottage varieties include *C.* 'Hagley Hybrid' (6 ft/2 m) with shell pink flowers with brown centers in summer; *C.* 'Jackmanii' (10 ft/3 m) has abundant velvety dark purple flowers in mid- and late summer; *C.* 'Vyvyan Pennell' (6-10 ft/2-3 m) has stunning double lavender blue flowers with a golden center. There are so many clematis to choose from, in such a wide variety of colors and forms, that it's best to visit a nursery and see what's available.

Cobaea scandens
CUP-AND-SAUCER PLANT
Height 16 ft/5 m
An interesting annual climber for warm yards, the cup-and-saucer plant is named for its bell-shaped flowers that spring from a distinct saucer-shaped cluster of leaves. The large creamy green flowers turn violet as they age, with a pleasant scent. *C. scandens alba* has pure white flowers, while *C. variegata* has variegated foliage. All species grow rapidly, making them ideal to cover a trellis or wigwam for "instant" height and impact.

Hydrangea anomala subsp. petiolaris
Height 40 ft/12 m
This is one of the best climbers for exposed, shady sites, thriving even on a cold north wall. It climbs via aerial roots, so it needs no training. Loose creamy-white domes of flowers appear in midsummer above clusters of dark green, oval leaves on pale green stems, which darken to a rich mahogany color when the spent flowers and leaves fall in the autumn.

Hedera helix
IVY
Height and Spread vary
Common ivy is an ancient plant that would have grown in the earliest country gardens. It is particularly valuable for growing on cold north-facing walls. Though it doesn't have much in the way of flowers, it attracts a range of wildlife for food and shelter — birds, bees, insects, even small mammals. Ivies grow in any soil; most are content in shade, but modern variegated types need some sunshine. Large-leaved yellow variegated types look dominant in a country garden, but green forms fit in anywhere.

Hedera helix

Humulus lupulus

HOPS

Height and Spread vary

This is another ancient plant, less widely grown than it merits, with very attractive pale green foliage and decorative papery fruits in the fall. Hops will grow in virtually any situation, but they are a bit rampant for a lot of yards, growing at least 15 feet (5 m) in one season, although you can keep cutting off the new shoots and eat them cooked like asparagus. The golden-leaved *H. lupulus aureus* has a more restrained habit. Grow it in full sun for the strongest color.

Ipomoea spp.

MORNING GLORY

Height 12 ft/4 m

Morning glories have always been popular in North America where they self-seed in many areas to spring up each year without help. In more northerly areas, they are grown as annuals, where their dramatic, late summer, large and brightly colored convolvulus-type flowers and huge floppy leaves provide a welcome show when other summer climbers are fading. They are very attractive grown up wigwams with beans, or through other climbers, and will flower prolifically in full sun. Each flower is short-lasting and closes into a tight furl in the afternoon to reopen as a generous trumpet in the morning, but the plants produce dozens of blooms in quick succession. *Ipomoea purpurea* has pink to blue flowers with white throats; *I. tricolor* 'Heavenly Blue' has rich bright blue flowers with white throats. If you can find it, *I. purpurea* 'Grandpa Ott' is a historic variety with deep purple blossoms and a bright yellow star in the throat. Morning glories grow rapidly, so you can sow them directly into the soil in early summer and still have a vibrant display by summer's end.

Jasminum spp.

JASMINE

Height varies

Try to find a suitable spot near the house or beside a sitting area for sweetly scented jasmine (*Jasminum officinale*), (height 30 ft/10 m) because its clusters of small, white, trumpet-shaped flowers are among the most intensely fragrant in any garden. Flowering from summer until early fall, jasmine is not completely hardy, so it needs a warm, sunny place. Early-summer-flowering *J. stephanense* has clusters of pale pink flowers on a slightly more compact plant with creamy yellow variegated leaves. The cheerful single yellow flowers and arching green shoots of winter-flowering jasmine (*Jasminum nudiflorum*) (height 10 ft/3 m) graced many a country garden, but this is a plant you either love or loathe, so take a good look at this evergreen shrub in other people's yards and see how you feel about it before planting. It is very useful in a cold or partly shaded site or in poor soil as it tolerates virtually any situation. It flowers on last year's wood, so trim it back well after flowering or it can get woody and straggly.

Lathyrus latifolius

EVERLASTING SWEET PEA

Height 6 ft/2 m

Another old favorite, grown in early country gardens, this reliable perennial produces swarms of pairs of purplish pink flowers all summer long. Although not strongly scented like its annual relative, it is a good-value, cheerful plant, particularly effective when growing through other shrubs or shrubby climbers to extend their flowering season and most attractive in the morning when the dew still glistens on its simple flowers. *L. grandiflorus* has stronger-colored red and purplish flowers. *L. nervosus*, 'Lord Anson's blue pea', is a rare perennial sweet pea with gloriously scented blue flowers. If you ever spot it, buy it immediately.

Lonicera periclymenum

HONEYSUCKLE

Height 22 ft/7 m

This trouble-free, vigorous, woody, British native is a must for every country garden, to cover walls, arches, or arbors. It's not the neatest of plants, but copes with ruthless cutting and tying to keep it in shape. In summer honeysuckle bears gloriously scented creamy white to yellow flowers, often flushed with reddish purple, darkening as they age to be followed by vivid red berries. *L. periclymenum* 'Belgica' produces reddish flowers fading to yellow in early summer; 'Serotina' has dark red-purple flowers in late summer. *L. japonica* varieties are evergreen or semi-evergreen; *L. japonica* 'Halliana' has very fragrant creamy yellow flowers appearing over a long period from spring to late summer, followed by blue-black berries. *L. fragrantissima,* winter honeysuckle, is also semi-evergreen, producing prolific quantities of scented creamy white flowers from late fall into spring if it is grown against a sheltered wall.

Magnolia x soulangeana

TULIP OR JAPANESE MAGNOLIA

Height and Spread 10 ft/3 m

You may have to wait five years or so before it flowers, but this magnolia makes a wonderful spreading wall shrub, producing pink-shaded purple flowers in mid- and late spring before its deep green leaves appear. It likes fairly heavy and slightly acid soil, and needs a sheltered spot where it is protected from strong spring sun, which browns frosted flowers. *M. grandiflora* has glossy deep green leaves with felted undersides and fragrant cream flowers throughout summer that are followed by green fruit pods. It will thrive in even alkaline soils. In cold areas it needs a sheltered wall in full sun or mid-shade, but it grows into a magnificent freestanding tree in warm places. You shouldn't need to prune magnolia, but if you want to shape it, trim carefully after it has finished flowering.

Parthenocissus quinquefolia

VIRGINIA CREEPER

Height 20 ft/6 m

This popular self-clinging climber has glossy, elegant, elongated ivy-shaped leaves that turn brilliant red in the fall. Most often grown on house walls, it is also excellent planted to clamber through evergreen trees, where its deep red foliage makes stunning early winter contrast. It is happiest in partial shade and tolerates most soils. *P. henryana* has hand-shaped leaves with distinct silver veins, turning purple-red in summer, then orange in the fall. It is excellent for a north wall in rich, moisture-retentive soil; plant it in a shady place to get the best leaf color.

Passiflora caerulea
PASSION FLOWER
Height 20 ft/6 m

If you grow a passion flower on a south-facing wall, it will make a very vigorous twining plant covered with flowers all summer. These flowers are exotically beautiful — a large flattened bowl of 3-4 inch (7-10 cm), blue-veined white flowers with a thick halo of blue-purple filaments surrounding the green anthers and prominent purple-topped stamens. Taken from their native South America to Europe in the 17th century, the strangely configured flowers led to all sorts of lore. Early papal scholars used the plants to help missionaries tell the Passion story to potential converts: they interpreted the petals as the apostles at the crucifixion of Jesus; the filaments were seen as the crown of thorns or halo; the anthers were the wounds; and the stigmas the nails. Passion flowers need a sunny, sheltered spot to thrive, but if you protect the base of a plant with straw or burlap over the winter, the plant should reappear the following year, even if it does get hit by frost. *P. caerulea* 'Grandiflora' has larger flowers, about 6 inches (15 cm) across, and *P. caerulea* 'Constance Elliott' has scented white flowers with pale blue or white filaments.

Tropaeolum speciosum
FLAME NASTURTIUM
Height 10 ft/3 m

It may take some time to get established, but this attractive perennial nasturtium produces long-spurred, bright vermilion red flowers during the summer. It needs to have its roots in shade in rich soil and looks particularly eye-catching peering through an evergreen holly or yew hedge.

Vitis vinifera purpurea
ORNAMENTAL GRAPE VINE
Height 20 ft/7 m

You can grow vines for wine in sunny country gardens, but for ornamental purposes choose varieties with large leaves and interesting fall coloring. The crimson-leafed ornamental vine has distinctive large-lobed leaves and produces handsome bunches of small black grapes in the fall, but these will be purely for show. *Vitis coignetiae,* the crimson glory vine, is a giant-leaved ornamental vine with heart-shaped toothed leaves that turn brilliant crimson in fall. Grow ornamental vines in partial shade for the best leaf color. They are happy in any free-draining garden soil.

Wisteria sinensis
WISTERIA
Height 30 ft/10 m

This climber was probably never grown in early country gardens. Reserved for rather grander houses, it is beautiful in any but the smallest yards, with its distinctive heavy pendants of bluish purple pealike flowers opening gradually in early summer among soft mid-green leaves and twining branches. A southwest-facing wall is best, but it will grow in any sheltered spot as long as the roots aren't restricted. Most people worry about pruning wisteria, but it's simple: to train the plant, tie the main shoots to a framework, chop them back to a third of their length in winter, and cut sideshoots back to two or three buds. Do this for up to five years until the plant is well established; then trim the plant to tidy it up if you need to after flowering and cut shoots as above in midwinter. If you get it wrong, don't worry. As a general rule it is always better to prune with a firm hand since it is very rare for a plant to die from overpruning, but they can become a bit of a nuisance if you are too tentative with your shears.

Passiflora caerulea

Vitis vinifera

Wisteria sinensis

Roses

Roses are essential to any country garden. In general, the older roses, with their slightly informal habits and old-fashioned flowers, look best in country gardens; modern Floribundas and Hybrid teas are rather too rigid and precise. Always choose scented roses — their fragrance is a vital part of their charm. The suggestions that follow give a tiny selection of all-time favorites, but the best way to choose is to visit a specialized nursery when roses are in bloom.

All roses like a sunny position in rich, moist, well-drained soil. Plant in spring or fall into very well-manured planting holes and mulch well in winter with more manure. In general, most roses can be cut back hard to about a third their size each winter once leaves have dropped. Make an angled cut above a healthy bud, keeping the centers of shrubby roses open and removing dead wood. Climbers can be pruned hard to maintain continued vigor, or minimally pruned to keep them in control, and ramblers should just be cut back to clean up straggly growth.

Most roses are bred to resist pests and diseases, although yellow varieties tend to be most susceptible. The best way to keep your roses free of aphids is to fill your yard with a variety of flowering plants to encourage pest predators, and blackspot will be discouraged by good maintenance and gardening practices, with late summer foliar feeding. It's accepted wisdom that you should never plant a new rose in the same place where one has been removed, but this need not be the case. If your soil is healthy and you dig a generous planting hole and backfill it well with manure and compost as you plant, you should have no problems.

Types of roses

Summer-flowering old roses give a magnificent display. Gallicas, once grown by Greeks and Romans, are the oldest known garden roses. They bear dark pink, red, or purplish single or double blossoms on hardy, compact plants. Many are richly fragrant. Damasks are another old group, believed to have been taken from the Middle East to Europe by Crusaders in the 12th century. Plants have loose arching branches, and flowers are usually pale pink and white, loose-petaled doubles and semi-doubles with intense perfume. Albas are strong and hardy plants, happy in most conditions. Leaves are blue-green, with fragrant pink

and white flowers. Centifolias are also known as cabbage roses because their many petals overlap rather like leaves of a cabbage. Plants are rather lax, and the rounded scented flowers range from white to deep pink. Moss roses developed from centifolias. Large, double, rounded flowers are intensely fragrant in white and shades of pink, red, or purple.

Repeat-flowering old roses include Chinas with small delicate flowers appearing all season on glossy, almost evergreen foliage. There are some very fragrant varieties, but China roses are slightly tender. Portlands are sturdy, upright plants with very fragrant double flowers that bloom all summer. Bourbons are very beautiful, with large highly fragrant flowers and growth habits ranging from slender and upright to very heavy and drooping. Hybrid perpetuals are strong, hardy, repeat-flowering plants with large fragrant blossoms. Another popular group for any garden is English roses, bred by the English grower David Austin from crosses between old roses and modern varieties; they look similar to old roses, with shrubby growth, and generally have rich fragrances.

Climbing roses generally repeat-flower after their first summer showing. There are climbing forms of many garden roses, their blossoms held singly or in small groups. Noisette roses are beautiful old climbers with small rosette flowers and long slender growth, but they are slightly tender, and need a warm wall and a sunny spot. Rambler roses tend to be more robust and faster-growing than most climbers, and flower freely but generally only once in the year. They are superb for rambling through bushes and into trees, and for covering large bare spaces quickly, and the less vigorous forms are excellent for covering arches and arbors even though they flower once only.

Rugosa roses are the least fussy of all roses, forming dense shapely shrubs with a mass of foliage and plenty of flowers early and late in summer, sometimes at the same time as their characteristic large hips. They will flourish even in poor sandy soil and don't need shelter, so they can make good hedging plants as well as shrubs in beds.

Rosa filipes 'Kiftsgate' is a glorious and prolific climbing rose that is covered with clusters of white flowers all summer. Plant with caution unless you have a large garden, as it must have plenty of space to ramble.

TOP TEN HEIRLOOM ROSES

R. x alba 'Cuisse de Nymph' or 'Great Maiden's Blush' was grown in the 15th century. It has double, soft pale pink flowers with a very strong sweet scent, and grayish foliage.

R. alba maxima is another 15th century rose with white flowers and gray-green foliage.

R. 'Cecile Brunner' is a 19th-century rose notable for its free-flowering habit producing scented, small, pink blooms over a long period. Shrubby and climbing forms are available.

R. centifolia is the original "cabbage rose." It forms a fragrant arching shrub with large, drooping, rounded flowers of clearest pink that open into many-petaled cups.

R. damascena 'Blush Damask' is a compact shrub rose, producing small, pale pink blossoms with deep pink centers and incredible scent.

R. damascena 'Trigintipetala' is a vigorous and reliable ancient rose with soft, warm blossoms with incredible scent.

Rosa filipes 'Kiftsgate' is a vigorous climber dating from the early 20th century.

Rosa gallica officinalis is the apothecary's rose from the Middle Ages.

Rosa gallica versicolor 'Rosa Mundi' is the oldest and best-known striped rose.

R. pimpinellifolia is an early flowering 15th-century Scotch rose.

Shrub roses

'Blanc Double de Coubert'
RUGOSA

Height and Spread 6 ft/2 m

This deservedly popular, reliable, pure white variety has beautiful large, semi-double, papery blossoms, produced from early summer until early fall. It is trouble-free in any situation except deep shade.

'Boule de Neige'
(BOURBON)

Height 5ft/1.6 m, Spread 3 ft/1 m

A favorite of many gardeners among pure white roses. The clusters of silky, white, camellia-like flowers produce an incredible perfume and bloom all summer. Plants have a slender growth habit and can be a little reluctant to get going, but persevere because these old roses are well worth the wait.

'Cardinal de Richelieu'
(GALLICA)

Height 4 ft/1.2 m, Spread 3 ft/1 m

Although this flowers only once in summer, its glorious scent and dusky rich wine red to purple flowers make this rose worthy of a place in any garden, where the blossoms will shine like jewels on summer mornings and evenings. Dark green foliage is almost thornless, so there's no excuse not to prune severely each year to guarantee the best display of flowers.

'Comte de Chambord'
(DAMASK)

Height 3 ft/1 m, Spread 2 ft/60 cm

This charming damask rose produces deliciously scented ruffled petals that open into flat, warm pink flowerheads. A very prolific flowerer, this is an ideal rose where space is limited, giving good value all summer.

'Ferdinand Pichard'
(HYBRID PERPETUAL)

Height and Spread 4 ft 6 in/1.5 m

This is a repeat-flowering striped rose with full, globular, deep pink flowers striped in purple and crimson. It is very striking in a country garden where its comparative lack of subtlety can be applauded rather than frowned upon.

'Gertrude Jekyll'
(ENGLISH ROSE)

Height and Spread 6 ft/2 m

Small scrolled buds expand into large, rich pink rosettes with a strong scent on this vigorous bushy plant.

'Graham Thomas'
(ENGLISH ROSE)

Height and Spread 4 ft/1.2 m

A reliable and trouble-free rose with a long flowering habit, the typical cabbage blooms of an older rose, and a sweet, strong scent similar to china roses. The pure yellow blossoms appear all summer above glossy mid-green leaves.

Rosa alba maxima
THE JACOBITE ROSE (ALBA)

Height 6 ft/2 m, Spread 4 ft 6 in/1.5m

This gloriously scented old garden rose must be included. It can often be found in neglected old country gardens because it survives in virtually any situation and soil, and needs little or no maintenance. Slightly untidy double white flowers open from pink buds in early summer on the fairly upright grayish leaved bush, spreading their heady scent before the blossoms of other roses are fully open. This rose was once the symbol of the House of York in the Wars of the Roses in 15th-century Britain.

Rosa californica plena
(SPECIES ROSE)

Height 8 ft/2.6 m, Spread 5 ft/1.5 m

This semi-double form of the wild R. californica makes an attractive back-of-the-bed shrub with its semi-double, deep pink flowers flopping forward on downward-arching stems. Their scent is delicious.

Rosa gallica officinalis
THE APOTHECARY'S ROSE (GALLICA)

Height and Spread 4 ft/1.2 m

This highly fragrant old rose has been grown for hundreds and possibly thousands of years for its wonderful strong scent. It produces masses of large, single, crimson flowers with golden stamens during midsummer, and is

Rosa gallica officinalis

Rosa gallica versicolor 'Rosa Mundi'

the sole source of petals recommended for herbalists' purposes. In the Wars of the Roses, *R. gallica officinalis* was adopted as the symbol of the House of Lancaster, but it was always as popular in humble English cottage gardens as in the grounds of Europe's grand castles and palaces.

Rosa gallica versicolor 'Rosa Mundi' (GALLICA)

Height and Spread 4 ft/1.2 m

This popular bushy rose must be planted in full sun to bring out its glorious scent, which will otherwise be rather restrained. Neat, semi-double blossoms have splashes of pink and purple on a dark pink background. It dates back to the 12th century and is believed to be named after Fair Rosamund, a mistress of England's King Henry II.

R. moyesii (SPECIES ROSE)

Height 10 ft/3 m, Spread 8 ft/2.6 m

This fine species rose has rich, blood red flowers reaching 3 inches (8 cm) across with golden stamens, followed by large, crimson, flagon-shaped hips in the fall. It forms a large open shrub with long arching branches, and is definitely worth growing if you have the space. Alternatively, try the more compact *R. moyesii* 'Geranium' (height and spread 7 ft/2.4 m), which produces similar flowers and even larger hips.

R. pimpinellifolia THE SCOTCH ROSE (SPECIES ROSE)

Height and Spread 3 ft/1 m

This attractive rose is ideal in beds where you want to grow a compact rose alongside plants that require less rich soil than roses generally tolerate. Pretty, open-faced, white flowers open in profusion all over the dense bush for two months in early summer. Although they have little scent, they are followed by striking, almost black hips, and plants are tough and tolerant of most conditions.

'Roseraie de l'Hay' (RUGOSA)

Height and Spread 7 ft /2.2 m

This vigorous rose has sturdy apple-green foliage out of which emerge gloriously rich port-wine-colored buds that open into wide (4-5 in./10-12 cm) crimson-purple blossoms. This rose seems completely pest and disease-free, and flowers reliably for months, producing a fantastic strong perfume.

'Souvenir de la Malmaison' (BOURBON)

Height and Spread 3 ft/1 m

Named after the Empress Josephine's famous rose garden, this is an intensely romantic shell pink rose. The large flowers open from soft cups into frilly quarters with a wonderful perfume all summer.

'William Lobb' (MOSS ROSE)

Height and Spread 6 ft/2 m

This robust rose flowers only once in summer, but it is definitely worth growing for its gloriously rich heady perfume and attractive reddish purple blossoms that eventually fade to a pleasing violet-grey.

Climbing roses

'Alchemist'

Height 12 ft/4 m

This robust, strongly fragrant, deep golden-orange rose flowers only once in early summer; it is particularly attractive planted with a later flowering variety of rose, a late-summer clematis, or even honeysuckle.

'Blairi No 2'

Height 15 ft/5 m

This stunning rose has deeply cupped, dense buds, dark pink in the middle, paler on the edges. It flowers prolifically once, followed by a few late flowers, and keeps its shape well with minimal pruning.

'Blush Noisette'

Height 12 ft/4 m

Grow this lilac pink, double-flowered rose for its glorious clove scent above all else. It is hardy and reliable, and blooms all summer long, and is particularly prolific against a sunny wall.

Rosa pimpinellifolia

Rosa 'Blanc Double de Coubert'

Rosa 'Alchemist'

'Gloire de Dijon'

Height 15 ft/5 m

A traditional old cottage-garden favorite, large pink- and gold-tinted buff yellow flowers with a strong fragrance are produced from early until late summer.

'Madame Grégoire Staechelin'

Height 20 ft/6.5 m

It flowers only once, but if you have space, you must include this magnificent rose, with its prolific clusters of generous semi-double flowers in clearest glowing pink that hang their heads to spread their lovely sweet-pea scent around the yard.

'Madame Alfred Carrière'

Height 20 ft/6.5 m

Another reliable and disease-resistant rose that will flourish in almost any position, even on a north wall. The delectably fragrant large cream blooms are tinted flesh pink, appearing all summer.

'Mermaid'

Height 25-30 ft/8-10 m

A good repeat-flowering rose with large, single, sulfur yellow petals and golden stamens. It is slightly tender but disease-resistant (unlike many yellow roses) and needs no pruning; just remove old wood in March.

'New Dawn'

Height 10 ft/3 m

This popular country-garden climbing rose with silvery pink flowers and glossy leaves blooms all summer. Well scented, it is a particularly good candidate for an arch, arbor or simple pergola.

'Sombreuil'

Height 12 ft/4 m

This prolifically flowering rose has a glorious scent and beautiful quartered blooms of creamy-white, sometimes tinted flesh pink at the center. It produces lots of lush green foliage to complement the flowers.

'Zéphirine Drouhin'

Height 12 ft/4 m

Each individual flower might not be spectacular, but en masse they are magnificent, fragrant deep rose-pink blooms produced in profusion all summer long. Fine in any position, this climber is particularly happy on a north wall and also makes a good hedging rose.

Rambling roses

'Albéric Barbier'

Height 25 ft/8 m

Wonderful strong rambler with glossy, almost evergreen foliage and clusters of yellow buds that open into creamy-white flowers in mid-June, with a reasonable second flowering in late summer. It is an ideal candidate for covering buildings or growing into trees.

'Albertine'

Height 20 ft/6.5 m

A very popular and reliable country-garden rambler, with strongly scented, russet-pink, double flowers.

R. banksiae 'Lutea'

Height 30 ft/9 m

Lightly fragrant, small, deep yellow flowers hang in sprays from this thornless rambler in early summer, before other roses are blooming. Ideal for an arbor or planted with a later flowering rose or other scented climber.

'Blush Rambler'

Height 12 ft (4 m)

Deliciously fragrant, small, blush-pink, cupped flowers hang in dense conical clusters in mid- to late summer. Vigorous yet neat, this is a good rambler for an arch or arbor.

'Félicité-Perpetué'

Height 20 ft/6.5 m

Large clusters of small, closely packed, creamy-white, pompom flowers follow pale pink buds in mid- to late summer, producing a strong, clear scent rather like primroses.

'Francis E. Lester'

Height 15 ft/5 m

Strongly fragrant, this rose has become increasingly popular since it appeared in the 1940s. It is hardy, and reliably smothered with huge bunches of small, blush-tinted white flowers in midsummer, followed by a mass of orange hips in the fall.

'Little Rambler'

Height 8 ft/2.5 m

A recent addition, the small, double pink flowers of this rose are intensely fragrant and fade to creamy-white with age. This rambler flowers repeatedly all summer, is hardy and disease-resistant, and a particularly good candidate to grow over an arch where you don't want growth to be too vigorous.

'Paul's Himalayan Musk'

Height 30 ft/10 m

Huge bunches of dainty, open-faced, blush pink roses with a glorious scent are produced on this wonderful rambler in early to midsummer, completely covering its long trailing growth. It rambles happily and rampantly, and looks particularly effective climbing through trees, from where it will hang down in long swathes once it reaches the top. It may be wise to check with your neighbors before planting this seductive rose along a boundary fence — it is impossible to restrain its vigor, but the more you chop it back, the happier it is.

'Rambling Rector'

Height 20 ft/6.5 m

Definitely a favorite for arbors. Small, open, creamy-white flowers with a delicious fragrance completely smother the short twiggy stems of this reliable rose. It also rambles happily into trees and over buildings.

Rosa 'Félicité-Perpetué

PRUNING ROSES

There is no mystery to pruning roses, but you must follow a few simple rules. Most important of all, always use sharp implements. Blunt tools damage the stems and encourage infection or cause the wood to die back, damaging the plant. The idea of pruning is to retain vigor and to maintain or develop a good shape. Some experienced gardeners nowadays prune rose bushes with a hedge trimmer, simply cutting everything back to about a third, but this tends to create rather square, uniform-shaped bushes. Beginners should always prune with sharp pruning shears or a pruning knife.

2 When you plant a new rose, always cut it back severely to leave no more than three or four healthy buds on each stem.

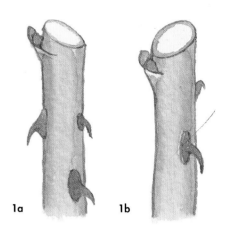

1a **1b**

1 Always prune as figure **1a** so that the cut is above a bud and sloping slightly away from it. Figure **1b** shows an incorrect cut where the cut slopes toward the bud.

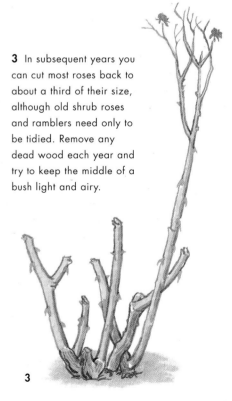

3 In subsequent years you can cut most roses back to about a third of their size, although old shrub roses and ramblers need only to be tidied. Remove any dead wood each year and try to keep the middle of a bush light and airy.

2

3

Bulbs and Corms

Some favorite old cottage flowers are bulbs. Bright tulips have always graced spring beds or stood proudly in tubs near the front door; lilies have been a feature of country gardens for centuries, and grape hyacinths have long been popular for that splash of deepest blue after dull winter days. A few daffodils and narcissus would probably have featured in many early gardens; fritillaries would have been tried early on, and members of the onion family have always been grown for their ornamental heads as well as their edible bulbs. Spring bulbs are particularly valuable in a small country garden, early sparks of cheerful color that take up virtually no space, poking out among the emerging foliage of perennial plants and dying back to allow summer flowers to come into their own. Most bulbs spread happily once established, and you should dig up clumps every three or four years after the leaves have died back and divide them, separating out the offsets — miniature bulbs produced by the parent plant. Or you can try growing bulbs from seed, under cover, ideally in a cool greenhouse, in the fall.

Allium sphaerocephalon

Allium spp.
ORNAMENTAL ONIONS
Height and Spread vary

Unless you are gardening on very heavy soil, you must include some alliums in your beds. All thrive in sunny, well-drained soil, and you can choose from delicate plants with open flowerheads to strong upright forms with huge round heads of globe-shaped clusters of tiny flowers. Tall varieties are slender plants, their flowers appearing on one erect stem above ground-level leaves so they take up little space but make a great impact when their showy heads peer out among stockier plants. In addition to being highly decorative, all alliums are believed to help the health of other neighboring plants, particularly roses, due to secretions from their roots. *Allium cernuum*, the nodding onion (height 15 in./37 cm, spread 8 in./20 cm) is a clump-forming variety, valued for its pretty linear foliage and loose clusters of pink-purple hanging flowers in midsummer. The elegant *A. azureum* (height 2 ft/60 cm) produces small compact heads of deepest cornflower-blue flowers in early to midsummer. *A. bulgaricum* (height 36-40 in./90-100 cm), an attractive variety producing loosely clustered, nodding heads of star-shaped bells of greenish-pink broadly striped with brownish red on the outside, flowers in early summer. *A. christophii* (height 18 in./45 cm) produces very large tight flowerheads of silvery-lilac starry flowers — they take up little space, so plant a generous number in your bed to look like a trail of shooting stars among other plants. *A. giganteum* (height 4-5 ft/1.2-1.5 m) produces huge purple globes 6 inches (15 cm) across in mid- to late summer. Plant allium bulbs 2-4 inches (5-10 cm) deep in the fall; they will spread themselves gradually through your beds as their bulbs increase, or they may self-seed.

Camassia spp.
QUAMASH
Height 18-48 in./45-120 cm, Spreads readily

Stunning in late spring and early summer, tall spikes of starry or cup-shaped bright blue or white flowers appear for several weeks on erect stems with small straplike leaves. Camassia will grow in sun or partial shade in deep, well-drained, fertile soil, and form generous clumps in a few years. *C. cusickii* (height 30-48 in./80-120 cm) has spires of pale to deep steel-blue flowers; *C. leichtlinii alba* (height 24-36 in./60-90 cm) has long spires of starry creamy-white flowers; *C. leichtlinii caerulea* flowers are deep blue. Plant bulbs in fall 4 inches (10 cm) deep.

Colchicum spp.
AUTUMN CROCUS, MEADOW SAFFRON, NAKED LADIES
Height 6-8 in./15-20 cm, Spreads readily

If you have an area of orchard, plant autumn crocus for their bright splashes of color in the grass beneath the trees. Clusters of flowers — large goblets in glowing shades of pinks, purples, and whites — emerge straight from the soil without leaves, on translucent pale green stems. The strap-shaped leaves only appear when the flowers are spent. Grown in gardens for centuries, colchicum were known as Naked Boys in the 17th century, and in the 18th century the leaves were valued for their production of colchicine, which was used in the treatment of gout — colchicine has since been found to be poisonous to humans and animals. Plant bulbs in summer 2-3 inches (5-8 cm) below the turf in dry, well-drained soil, in full sun or light shade.

Cyclamen spp.
CYCLAMEN
Height 4-6 in./10-15 cm, Spread 6 in./15 cm
Strictly tuberous perennials grown from corms rather than bulbs, *Cyclamen coum* produce pinkish red or white flowers on russet brown, wiry stems above mounds of dark green heart-shaped leaves in winter or early spring. They will flower in the open, but are best in partial shade. Plant the corms in late summer into rich, well-drained soil, ideally under trees or shrubs, and topdress them with manure or compost once leaves die down in late spring. *Cyclamen neapolitanum* (syn. *hederifolium*) produce deep rose-pink flowers with a dark eye on stiff dark reddish brown stems in mid- and late autumn, followed by glossy triangular to heart-shaped leaves blotched and marbled with lighter green. *C. neapolitanum album* has pure white flowers, followed by silver marbled leaves. After flowering, the long stems curl to throw their seeds around freely to make new plants in shady, compost-rich soil — they grow particularly well under deciduous trees where soil is enriched with leaf mold.

Erythronium dens-canis
DOGS' TOOTH VIOLET
Height 12 in./30 cm, Spreads readily
Ideal for a shady bed or beneath a spreading tree, this plant was popular in British cottage gardens by the 17th century. It has bright green leaves mottled with darker green and brown, and produces white or pinkish lilac flowers with reflex petals that turn back from the purple anthers. Plant bulbs 4 inches (10 cm) deep in the fall in a semi-shady spot in deep, moist, but well-drained soil, and divide mature clumps immediately after they have flowered in spring.

Fritillaria imperialis
CROWN IMPERIAL
Height 20-36 in./48-90 cm, Spread 18 in./45 cm
A good old cottage-garden favorite grown since the 16th century, fritillaria has large heads of yellow or orange bell-shaped flowers that appear in late spring on sturdy stems topped by a tuft of green leaves. Crown imperials like rich deep soil and must be planted deeply. They enjoy rather alkaline lime-rich soil best, but will put on a reasonable show in most soils, content in sun and partial shade. 'Rubra Maxima' is a good dark red variety. Snakeshead fritillaries *Fritillaria meleagris* (height 10 in./25 cm) are delicate plants most often used to naturalize in grass, but also very appealing peering out from among other foliage on the edge of sunny or shady beds. Nodding bells are checkered deep purple and white, or pure white. They were named checkered daffodils or ginnea-hen flowers when they first appeared in Europe in the 16th century. They spread well after a few years but are often mistakenly dug up with over-zealous weeding when planted in beds — they look like grass when not in flower.

Galanthus nivalis
SNOWDROP
Height 4-10 in./10-25 cm, Spreads readily
The common snowdrop has been grown throughout Europe for centuries, but the great enthusiasm for snowdrops really took off in the 19th century. Since then, they have become indispensable spring flowers in any yard. Delightful planted in grass, they are just as good in shady beds, and pretty in pots. Although snowdrops are bulbs, they are best planted "in the green" in late spring after they have

Camassia cusickii

Cyclamen neapolitanum

Fritillaria meleagris

flowered; spread them by dividing clumps every three years.

Hyacinthoides non-scripta

BLUEBELL

Height 12 in./30 cm, Spreads rapidly

You must include at least one generous clump of bluebells, with their packed spires of delicately scented, blue, bell-shaped flowers in late spring and early summer. Having graced patches of shady wasteland and woodland in Europe for thousands of years, they came early into country gardens. They are easy to grow in any reasonably fertile soil, excellent for naturalizing in orchards and wild gardens, and bring color to beds in spring. Plant bulbs 2-4 inches (5-10 cm) deep in the fall.

Lilium spp.

LILIES

Height and Spread vary

There are dozens of beautiful lilies, old and new, but a few have been cottage-garden favorites for hundreds of years. The turkscap or martagon lily (L. martagon) (height 4 ft/ 1.2 m) is an ancient country-garden variety, very easy to establish in any sunny spot and well-drained soil, producing a mass of pink flowers all up the stems, the petals turned back like turbans. The strikingly beautiful Madonna lily (L. candidum) (3-5 ft/90 cm-1.5 m) was growing in European cottage gardens by the 14th century and continues to be justifiably popular with its wonderfully scented pure white flowers wafting their sweet fragrance about the yard in summer. Unfortunately, it is slightly temperamental, requiring three months of good sunshine to flower well, and bulbs must never be covered with more than 1 inch (2.5 cm) of soil. Plant bulbs in a sunny spot in rich, moisture-retentive soil in the fall. The regal lily L. regale (height 6 ft/2 m) is a relative newcomer, appearing in country gardens at the end of the 19th century, but it flowers prolifically with up to 20 fragrant and beautiful white trumpet flowers on each stem, stained with pinkish purple on the outside. It is similarly striking to the Madonna lily but much more reliable. L. tigrinum (height 6 ft/1.8 m) is the tiger lily, whose black-spotted orange flowers are longstanding favorites, but have no scent. Lilies, apart from Madonna lilies, should be planted in the fall or spring about 4-6 inches (10-15 cm) deep among herbaceous plants where their roots will be shaded but their heads will be in the sun. They need rich soil, but it must drain well or bulbs will rot.

Muscari spp.

GRAPE HYACINTHS

Height 6 in./15 cm, Spreads readily

Perfect cheerful and unassuming cottage-garden plants, the spires of bright blue flowers on short compact plants are easy to grow from fall-planted bulbs, spread rapidly, and look charming along the edges of paths and in the fronts of beds in a country garden. They are also excellent planted in pots with early tulips for a grand splash of color. Once planted, they'll spread whatever you do, although like all bulbs, they are happiest if lifted and divided fairly regularly.

Narcissus spp.

DAFFODILS AND NARCISSUS

Height and Spread vary

Daffodils are wonderful in large gardens, but frankly rather irritating in small spaces: they need deadheading if you don't cut them for the house or they look rather hideous, and their foliage hangs around untidily for ages after the pretty flowers have faded. However, if you love them, you must have them, and there are hundreds of varieties to choose from. Bulbs should be planted in the fall 3-4 inches (8-10 cm) deep in any well-drained soil, in sun or partial shade, and plants must be divided every three years or so after flowering. Among the older varieties that found their way early into country gardens are N. pseudonarcissus, the Lent lily or wild daffodil (height 8-12 in./20-30 cm), with very erect leaves and small yellow trumpets with smaller pale yellow or cream petals surrounding them. N. poeticus 'Plenus' (16 in./40 cm) produces fragrant, snowy white, open-faced flowers with tiny red-tipped cups. N. poeticus 'Plenus' var. recurvus has curved-back glistening white petals and red-tipped cups; its common name is Old Pheasant's Eye.

Lilium regale

Narcissus poeticus 'Plenus'

Tulipa spp.

TULIPS

Height and Spread vary

One of the hallmarks of country gardens, bright tulips must be included in tubs and beds. There are thousands of types to choose from nowadays, but do include the good old-fashioned bright red or yellow cottage tulip before moving on to some of the wonderful ruffled, striped, and splashed tulips in a glorious choice of colors. It's best — and very pleasant — to pore over a specialized catalog in summer to order your personal favorites for fall planting. You can choose tulips to flower continuously from early spring for three months, but all must be planted 4-5 inches (10-12 cm) deep in well-drained soil in late fall. The bulbs need baking in the sun to keep flowering well, so they need a sunny spot without too much encroaching foliage, or you will need to replace the bulbs every few years. Some gardeners counsel lifting tulips every year after the leaves have died back, but this shouldn't be necessary if they are planted in an appropriate spot. Early-flowering species certainly need never be lifted, and sturdy cottage tulips should last well. However, if you plant tulips for bright displays in containers, plant them in a gritty potting mixture and lift them after the foliage has died back. Then store them in a dry cool place to replant late the following fall.

The earliest flowering tulips are the short-stemmed (6-8 in./15-20 cm) Kaufmanniana species, then come Fosteriana and Greigii (8-18 in./20-45 cm), followed by compact Single Early and Double Early tulips (up to 15 in./ 40 cm). Triumph tulips are taller midseason forms (12-20 in./30-50 cm); then come Darwin hybrids, stately Cottage tulips (18-26 in./45-65 cm), and finally Lily and Parrot, Viridiflora, and Late Peony tulips (18-24 in./45-60 cm). Everyone has their favorites, including pure white 'Purissima' Kaufmanniana, the stately dark purple 'Queen of the Night' cottage tulip, and the strong-stemmed, large-flowered, frilly, mauve 'Blue Parrot.'

A cheerful combination of red tulips and bright yellow wallflowers.

Herbs

Herbs were the early country gardener's flowers and medicines, important in the house to use as air fresheners and insect repellents as well as for flavorings in the kitchen. Herbs should still be an important part of every country garden, for use and decoration, and to improve the health of the garden since they make excellent companions for many other plants. Many are very attractive and smell deliciously fragrant, and most are extremely easy to grow with virtually no maintenance. You can grow some herbs in even rather damp, shady places, but many favorites originate from the Mediterranean and grow best in a sunny spot on well-drained, light soil. Most are also extremely happy growing in containers, so cluster a few in a sunny spot near the back door where you can easily pick a handful for the kitchen.

A broad ribbon of sage provides good color and structure in an herb bed among smaller leaved herbs.

Allium schoenoprasum

CHIVES

Height 6 in./15 cm

A must for every country garden, this versatile herb can be used to edge paths or herb beds. It is a perfect companion for roses, where it helps to repel aphids and may even prevent blackspot, and it is a useful flavoring and salad addition. Moreover, the plants are very fast growing and perennial, needing only to be divided and replanted in mid-spring. Chives need a rich, moist soil for the most succulent leaves, but flower most freely on poor, slightly acidic soil.

Anethum graveolens

DILL

Height 24-48 in./60-120 cm

A welcome addition to any garden, either among other herbs, in beds, or even in the vegetable plot. Once used as a talisman against witchcraft, it is an excellent aid to digestion, and the leaves are delicious in salads or with fish. Dill has pretty, feathery, blue-green foliage and large, flat, yellow flowerheads in late summer that ripen into small caraway-flavored seeds. It also attracts beneficial insects to the garden. Sow seeds in late spring in a sunny sheltered spot where you want them to grow.

Anthriscus cerefolium

CHERVIL

Height 24 in./60 cm

Hardy chervil grows in sun or partial shade in any moisture-retentive soil, with delicate white flowers in spring and deeply cut, attractive, sweetly scented foliage. It has a slightly aniseed flavor and is delicious in soups and stews or omelets, one of the classic *fines herbes* of French cooking. Sow seeds in spring and fall for year-round plants, where weather permits. In colder climates sow seeds successively in summer for a continuous crop until frost.

Artemisia dracunculus

FRENCH TARRAGON

Height 24-36 in./60-90 cm

Although French tarragon is related to the native wormwood *Artemisia absinthum,* grown in the earliest country gardens, the two have very different characters. Hardy wormwood was grown thousands of years ago as a healing herb in Britain and makes an attractive decorative plant with its deeply cut, downy, silvery gray leaves and distinctive scent. French tarragon, a staple of European cooking for centuries, has long, narrow, dark green leaves and is slightly tender, so it must be replanted each year. It doesn't set seed in cooler climates, so grow in sunny well-drained soil from seedlings purchased from a reputable supplier — beware of the coarser Russian tarragon, which is a tougher-looking plant, fully hardy but with virtually no flavor.

Borago officinalis

BORAGE

Height 12-24 in./30-60 cm

Borage is an easy, decorative annual herb with lovely blue flowers which brighten up the garden even if you never use the plant as a tonic like earlier country gardeners. It germinates easily, so just push a few seeds into the soil after the last frost. It will grow in moist shade as well as sunny situations. Once established, borage self-seeds to romp freely around the garden, attracting bees and generally lifting the spirits. Historically, borage was reputed to cheer melancholy and to encourage a positive outlook, and research has shown it contains substances that may affect the hormones, supporting the ancient beliefs in its properties.

Coriandrum sativum

CORIANDER

Height 18-24 in./45-60 cm

Coriander has been widely grown for centuries, originally used as a tonic and aphrodisiac and to flavor roast meat, but now grown as a vital ingredient in Indian and Latin-American cooking. It is an attractive, feathery-leaved herb, rather like flat-leaved parsley, with a delicious spicy scent. Sow seeds in late spring or early summer into deep rich soil in a sunny position, and keep cutting plants hard to prevent them

Anethum graveolens

Anthriscus cerefolium

Borago officinalis

from flowering — although the small white flowers are attractive. For a continuous crop until frosts in the fall, sow several times through summer, watering seedlings well.

Foeniculum vulgare
FENNEL
Height 3-6 ft/1-2 m

This statuesque but graceful perennial is one of the oldest known kitchen herbs, its seeds and leaves widely used in fish dishes, sauces, and vegetables. Grow it as a centerpiece to any herb bed or among your flowers, for its feathery foliage makes a fine bright green clump with generous, yellow, umbrella-shaped flowerheads that produce thousands of dark seeds. Young shoots can be eaten as a vegetable or added to salads. Sow seed in a sunny position in moist soil in mid-spring and cut it right back to the ground in the fall when you have harvested the seeds. You can also grow it as an annual.

Galium odorata
WOODRUFF
Height 6-10 in./15-25 cm

Not much grown nowadays, white-flowered and square-stalked perennial woodruff is odorless when it is fresh but has a fragrant haylike scent when dried. It used to be used as a "strewing" herb to sweeten the air of Tudor houses and churches, and wreaths and sprigs of dried woodruff were placed in drawers and bedding to freshen textiles and remove musty smells. Try growing it to use as an air freshener today; it is much pleasanter than any chemical preparation in a bottle. Woodruff will grow as groundcover in moist shade or partial shade. Plant stem cuttings in the fall or spring.

Hyssopus officinalis
HYSSOP
Height 24 in./60 cm

Hyssop is a hardy evergreen perennial with woody stems, small, pointed, pungently fragrant leaves and spikes of deep blue or pink flowers. Sow seeds in spring into light well-drained soil in full sun, or raise it from softwood cuttings. Its dense bushy habit makes hyssop a good plant for low hedging around an herb bed or to edge a vegetable plot because the flowers attract all sorts of beneficial insects as well as being a magnet for bees. Hyssop was traditionally grown in country gardens for use in a tonic to ease coughs and colds, as well as for ornament; leaves also make a pleasant addition to salads or when roasting fatty meats.

Inula helenium
ELECAMPANE
Height 4-5 ft/1.2-1.5 m

Perennial elecampane was once grown very widely, its root used in many country medicines. It has slightly downy gray-green leaves and bright yellow flowers that look like miniature sunflowers. It is very attractive among vegetables or allowed to self-seed in sun or partial shade in any moist conditions.

Laurus nobilis
BAY, SWEET BAY
Height 8 ft/2.4m

Although bay is a tender Mediterranean plant, it was growing in grand gardens in Britain from the 11th century, and soon found its way into humbler gardens. It was used as a hedging plant in south- or southwest-facing sunny gardens, or less commonly in tubs that could be moved into shelter in winter. It is a good plant for clipping into shapes such as standard balls or pyramids. The leaves are useful in so many dishes that it's worth growing bay even if your garden is rather cool. Either plant in a container and move it into a porch or greenhouse for winter, depending on your climate, or wrap the whole plant in bubble wrap, or more traditionally straw, and cover the package with burlap, opening it up again in early spring, and remembering to keep it protected from any frosts. Grow bay from cuttings or nursery stock, planted in rich well-drained soil. If you decide to grow a bay tree in a container, use a mixture of two-thirds good potting mixture and one-third soil, and be sure to keep young plants well watered.

Lavandula spp.
LAVENDER
Height 12-24 in./30-60 cm

It is hard to imagine a country garden without sweetly scented lavender glowing mauve-blue in summer, surrounded by buzzing insects. Old English lavender (Lavandula angustifolia, sometimes referred to as L. spica, L. vera, or L. officinalis) appeared in the earliest country gardens, from seeds and slips brought back from grander gardens elsewhere. Its generous gray foliage and copious blue flowers are strongly fragrant and loved by gardeners, bees, and insects alike. Depending on the planting recommendation for your area, sow seeds in spring or fall into well-drained fertile soil in full sun, or propagate from softwood cuttings in summer. Keep lavender well trimmed to maintain a good shape and prevent it from getting woody or straggly. Cut plants back in spring to within 2 inches (5 cm) of the old wood, then trim after flowering if necessary to tidy plants. Try not to neglect plants, as they seldom regrow if pruned right back to old wood. Lavender is a good subject to be clipped into balls or other simple shapes; if you grow it as a low hedge, clip it into rounded mounds. You can find pink and white forms of Lavandula angustifolia, but none seem quite so prolific or hardy. There are dozens of forms of lavender, with variable foliage from very gray, hard, short leaves and twiggy branches to arching branches with much softer foliage in shades from gray to medium green. In general, the softer the foliage, the more tender the variety. L. 'Munstead' is the best variety for a dwarf hedge, good for edging an herb garden or the front of a bed with good lavender flowers and very neat, hard foliage. 'Nana Alba' is a good white dwarf form. French lavender (L. stoechas) is a lovely herb in a sunny garden, slightly tender, with soft gray-green foliage. In colder areas grow it in containers to be moved under cover in winter. It produces very upright, fluffy flowers in lavender-blue, white, or pink with petals protruding from the top like rabbit's ears. Trim French lavender after flowering.

Levisticum officinale

LOVAGE

Height 5 ft/1.5 m

This tall hardy perennial is grown for its attractive deep green leaves, tasting of celery or aniseed and delicious for flavoring many foods. It flourishes happily in moist, deep soil in partial shade, and can be grown from seed in spring. Or plant nursery-grown seedlings — once established, it will self-seed if you let it and is a good addition to a flower or a vegetable bed. Cut plants back to the ground in winter.

Matricaria chamomilla

GERMAN CHAMOMILE OR SCENTED MAYWEED

Height 6-18 in./15-45 cm)

A hardy annual with domed, white, pineapple-scented, daisylike flowers on slender stems with a few deeply cut, dark green leaves. Grown for centuries, the flowers make an excellent herbal tea and can be used in salves and ointments. Roman chamomile *(Chamamaelum nobilis)* is a creeping species, more strongly scented with a mat of feathery gray-green foliage above which rise white daisylike blossoms in midsummer.

C. nobilis 'Treneague' is used for chamomile lawns and seats because it does not flower.

Melissa officinalis

LEMON BALM

Height 24 in./60 cm

Many old country gardens contain lemon balm, because once this hardy fragrant perennial is planted, it spreads vigorously. Easily grown from seed in any conditions, the scent is strongest when grown in moist soil in a sunny position. To keep it in check, plant in a large pot or bucket sunk into the soil, and prune regularly to maintain a neat bushy habit. Its small white flowers are much loved by bees, and the lemony leaves can be steeped to make Melissa tea, a headache remedy and general pick-me-up.

Mentha spp.

MINT

Height 8-15 in./20-36 cm

There are mints to suit all tastes, including common mint, spearmint, apple mint, and ginger mint. Every garden must include some of this family, invaluable in cooking and for brewing soothing teas, but it's always best to grow them in containers sunk into the earth, not in open ground where they can spread invasively. Mints prefer moist soil and a shady or semi-shady spot, but they'll grow anywhere from a tiny piece of root — mints root easily. Place a sprig in a glass of water, and it will have formed a root ready to plant within a week or two. Pennyroyal *(Mentha pulegium)* is one of the best deterrents for mice and ants, so plant it in vegetable and flower beds if you have trouble with pests.

Myrrhis odorata

SWEET CICELY

Height 24-36 in./60-90 cm

This perennial, cool-climate herb resembles a more elegant, compact, Queen Anne's lace, very decorative with its lacy foliage and flat heads of white flowers in late spring followed by crowns of black seeds, which were crushed and used as a flavoring in cordials and drinks. Its leaves sweeten sour fruits and flavor butter. It requires a partially shaded position and deep, moist, compost-rich soil to flourish, and will not flower in hot climates. Sow seeds in late summer or fall, and thin choice seedlings in spring into a deep bed because sweet cicely has a long taproot.

Lavandula angustifolia 'Hidcote'

Melissa officinalis variegata

Mentha rotundifolia

Myrtus communis

MYRTLE

Height 36 in./90 cm, Spread 24 in./60 cm

Evergreen myrtle forms an attractive bush with highly scented white summer flowers followed by black berries and glossy dark green leaves that give off a delicious fragrance when bruised. It is a little tender so it needs a sunny site in well-drained, light, fertile soil, but it was a traditional country-garden plant, placed near the front door so newlyweds would live in love and peace. It is included in bridal bouquets through much of southern Europe and in Britain, where royal brides carry a sprig from a bush grown from a piece of myrtle in Queen Victoria's wedding wreath. Grow it for its scent, its looks, and its associations, and protect it from frosts. If leaves do get scorched, the plant will usually recover; just trim back all the frost damage in spring. Myrtle makes a lovely subject for topiary in sheltered gardens.

Ocimum basilicum

BASIL

Height 10 in./25 cm

This tender aromatic herb is an essential

Ocimum basilicum

ingredient for many summer dishes. You may find it best to grow it in containers of good garden soil or in sunny windowboxes instead of open ground, because it is a magnet for slugs and needs a warm, sunny summer. Sow sweet basil seeds indoors, and plant them out into well-drained fertile soil in early summer, hardening them off well beforehand. Protect vulnerable young seedlings from slugs by surrounding them with gritty barriers and covering them with cut-off plastic bottles or cloches. Water plants regularly, remove flower stalks as soon as they appear to prolong leaf growth, and pinch out tops regularly to promote bushy growth. Purple basil has attractive reddish-purple foliage, but is slightly more tender than the green form. Greek basil has smaller leaves than sweet basil; keep trimming the bushes for a long crop. The leaves of Thai basil have a slightly spicy flavor.

Origanum vulgare

MARJORAM

Height 10-24 in./25-60 cm

This ancient herb was once used as a fairly universal healer, reputedly curing ailments as varied as rheumatism and toothache, colds and hayfever. It was an essential flavoring for meat in Elizabethan England and a popular salad herb for centuries. Nowadays this perennial herb is also deservedly popular in tomato dishes. It prefers a sunny spot and well-drained fertile soil; you can either sow seed in spring, propagate from stem cuttings, or get a clump from a friend who is dividing theirs. *Origanum vulgare* 'Aureum' is an attractive golden-leaved variety, but plant it in semi-shade or the leaves may scorch. *Origanum onites* is tender and should be grown as an annual in cool climates; it is as essential as basil in Italian dishes.

Petroselinum crispum

PARSLEY

Height 6 in./15 cm

Another garden essential, parsley has been grown in country gardens for centuries, with plenty of folklore to accompany it. It was once considered that good women could not grow parsley successfully, a flourishing crop implied the woman of the house was a witch — probably a relict of the herb's pre-medieval reputation as a poisonous plant. It was considered dangerous to transplant parsley or it would cause deaths in the family, and it was one of the many plants that lore suggested should only be sown on Good Friday when the devil couldn't affect it. Parsley is deep rooted and flourishes in a rich, moist, vegetable bed. The seed can be slow to germinate, so an old trick is to pour boiling water onto a seed drill when you sow the seed in late spring. Flat-leaved parsley is increasingly popular and germinates more readily than the traditional curly-leafed variety.

Rosmarinus officinalis

ROSEMARY

Height and Spread 18-40 in./45-100 cm

Another essential, long grown in country gardens and used to flavor meat and poultry, and also once employed as a charm to lure sweethearts, to protect the house from malign spirits, and as an herb of remembrance.

Petroselinum crispum

Deliciously scented woody shrubs have gray-green leaves, and the shrubby bushes are covered with blue flowers in spring or early summer, depending on variety. Grow rosemary in a sunny position in well-drained soil, from softwood cuttings or nursery stock. There are ornamental upright or prostrate forms, with flower color ranging from dark to pale blue, and pink and white forms, but the best flavor for cooking comes from the traditional shrubby variety. Rosemary is a good subject for simple topiary, and makes a fine hedge, particularly near the ocean since it is very tolerant of salt.

Ruta graveolens
RUE
Height and Spread 12-36 in./30-90 cm

Not everyone likes the musky smell of rue, but it has been grown for centuries, with its attractive blue-green rounded leaves and yellow flowers. It repels many pests, from insects to dogs, and used to be planted as a defense against witches. Grow it in a sunny spot in well-drained soil, but keep it well away from strawberries or tomatoes, which seem to hate it.

Salvia officinalis
SAGE
Height 12-24 in./30-60 cm, Spread 24-36 in./60-90 cm

Sage is a strong-smelling hardy perennial shrub, with dusky green felted leaves, although foliage can also be purple, or splashed with pink, cream, and white. Small, purplish blue flowers appear on spires in late summer. Grow sage from cuttings in well-drained soil in full sun, cut it back hard after flowering to encourage new young shoots. You may need to protect plants from winter frosts by covering them with burlap. Use sage leaves in cooking and in teas and infusions as a simple but effective throat remedy.

Satureja spp.
SAVORY
Height and Spread 12-18 in./30-45 cm

Summer savory (Satureja hortensis) is a bushy, low-growing annual with narrow, dark green scented leaves and whorls of rather insignificant pink or blue and white flowers that bees love. The leaves taste strongest before the plants flower, so keep it trimmed to prolong leafy growth and delay flowering. Traditionally a companion plant for broad beans, sow seeds into light, moisture-retentive soil in late spring. Savory was used for centuries to cure flatulence, and the peppery chopped leaves are a delicious accompaniment to beans, peas, and legumes. Winter savory (Satureja montana) is a slightly smaller perennial herb with woody branching stems, very similar in appearance to summer savory, but with a slightly more bitter scent and flavor. Grow one or two plants as evergreen bushes in warm gardens.

Symphytum officinale
COMFREY
Height 40 in./100 cm, Spread 30 in./80cm

Comfrey is a sturdy hardy perennial frequently found growing wild along roadsides but less common in herb gardens, although Russian comfrey cultivars should be grown in any garden because they are invaluable in the compost heap, a rich source of minerals, and the steeped or rotted leaves make a rich fertilizer. Comfrey would have been grown in all early country gardens for its healing properties as well as its flowers — attractive drooping bells of mauve, blue, or white on slender stems. It has remarkable power to repair bruises and heal tissue, and used to be called knitbone for its ability to heal breaks and sprains when used as a compress.

Tanacetum parthenium
FEVERFEW
Height 18 in./45 cm

Feverfew's daisy flowers and attractive chrysanthemum-like leaves make it easy to place in any garden, in light well-drained soil. It was grown in early country gardens among the flowers and vegetables and to edge beds. Although perennial, it is short-lived and best grown as an annual. Sow seeds in spring after frost. Feverfew is still one of the best remedies for migraines, but the leaves taste very bitter, so sandwich them between bread with a sprinkling of sugar to make the remedy more palatable.

Tanacetum vulgare
TANSY
Height 24-36 in./60-90 cm

Tansy is another old English herb. Its leaves were a favorite flavoring in custards and other sweet puddings in the Middle Ages and again in Victorian times, and it has been widely used in fish dishes and meat stuffings. It is an attractive plant with masses of long-lasting, yellow, button-shaped flowers in summer above ferny leaves, and is now generally grown for ornament and for cutting and drying rather than for use in the kitchen. It is a good plant to fill a slightly shady spot or a corner with poor soil because tansy will happily grow in any condition, tolerating shade as much as it enjoys sun and throwing out masses of deep yellow heads all summer. Beware of its invasive habit; in a small yard it is best to grow tansy in a container.

Thymus vulgaris
THYME
Height 6-12 in./15-30 cm

Essential for the kitchen, intensely fragrant thyme has been cultivated since the days of ancient Greece and grows wild in many warm climates. Long considered an herb that promoted sleep, it is still used in herb pillows and made into an infusion to relieve exhaustion and headaches. In the kitchen it is used as a flavoring for many meat, fish and vegetable dishes, soups and stews, and makes an excellent herb vinegar. Thyme needs to be grown in full sun and very well-drained soil; it will die very quickly if its feet get wet. Sow seed in the fall or spring, or plant stem cuttings or nursery-grown stock. Keep it cut back well to encourage plants to form bushy mats and to stop it from getting woody, but you will probably still need to replace thyme every three or four years. Common thyme is best for cooking.

Vegetables

Try to follow country garden tradition and grow some vegetables, whatever size your garden is. In a small space, grow a few favorites in sunny beds, perhaps scattering lettuce seeds in small patches, or include dramatic-colored chards or striking statuesque artichokes to complement your flowers. Early cottage gardeners had no hesitation in mixing their vegetables with poppies and marigolds and other bright herbs and flowers, and even a plot dedicated to vegetables should include a scattering of poppies and herbs around the edges to encourage pest predators and generally help your vegetables' health. When you plant in your beds, scatter a large handful of compost onto the soil every time you sow or harvest a vegetable to keep the soil fertile.

Vegetables need a reasonable measure of sun. None except rhubarb will grow in deep shade, but a partially shaded plot is fine for most leafy greens and brassicas. However, tender vegetables such as tomatoes, corn, and peppers won't ever be productive in shade. If possible, divide a vegetable plot roughly into four so you can rotate crops to keep the soil healthy, and add as much organic matter and manure as possible to the vegetable garden (see page 37). Crops were traditionally planted in rows, but planting in blocks saves space on access paths, and vegetables are easier to harvest without treading too much on the soil, which compacts it and breaks down the structure, reducing fertility. Some gardeners like to make slightly raised beds about 4 feet (1.2 m) wide for maximum productivity, since you can plant your vegetables closer together in deeper beds, and once you've made the beds, you never need to step on the soil again.

Restrained by neatly clipped low box hedging, a bean wigwam rises from a leafy jungle of ruby chard.

TOP SALAD LEAVES

Arugula

Peppery leaves that can be picked from spring to early winter with successive sowings. Keep well watered and keep picking to prevent bolting. Although perennial, it is best to sow seed every spring and summer; you will have leaves to pick within 3 weeks.

Cut-and-come-again lettuce

Cut when 2-4 inches (5-10 cm) tall (3-4 weeks after sowing); leaves resprout for a second or third cutting. You can sow throughout the season, but lettuce seed doesn't germinate at high temperatures; midsummer sowings may bolt or become coarse. Keep well watered. Best varieties: red and green Salad Bowl, Lollo Rossa.

Mache/corn salad

Low-growing, small, dark green rosettes that grow virtually all year round in mild climates, providing salad leaves in winter. Sow seeds in spring in partial shade; mache bolts quickly in a sunny position.

Mizuna

An Oriental green with dark, glossy, serrated leaves with narrow white stalks that grows well in cool climates, even in winter if it's not too wet, cold, or snowy. Pick leaves when young and they will resprout.

Nasturtium

Nasturtium leaves are peppery and delicious, great in a mixed salad bowl; the flowers are very tasty, too, as well as decorative.

Sorrel

These lance-shaped bright green leaves taste sharp and lemony. Sow in late spring in sun or partial shade; keep well watered. Leaves are best in spring and early summer, then again in fall.

Spicy greens

Sow packets of mixed spicy greens (colored mustards and Russian red kale) for early and late season salad greens, cutting them when 4-5 inches (10-12 cm) tall. They will resprout several times.

Allium cepa
ONIONS

Height 12-18 in./30-45 cm

Onions need fertile, well-drained soil and a long growing season to produce large bulbs. You can either sow seed indoors in a warm place in early spring for planting in mid- to late spring or plant onion sets — small bulblets — in spring as soon as the ground is workable. The growth of bulb onions depends on day-length; leaf growth stops by midsummer when days start to shorten, and after that the bulbs start to swell. They can be pulled for use at any stage and can be dried for storage once the foliage has died back in late summer. Leave them for a couple of weeks before lifting and leaving them to dry thoroughly. Onion beds must be kept weed free, and rotation is particularly important to avoid possible buildup in the soil of the grubs of onion maggot or of diseases such as white rot. Keep pests off onions by covering the crop with floating row covers when they are most susceptible in early summer; infested plants should be dug up and disposed of outside the garden. If white rot appears as silver streaks on the foliage in cool damp summers, lift affected onions immediately; they cannot be stored.

Allium porrum
LEEKS

Height 12-18 in./30-45 cm

Leeks are a hardy winter vegetable, thriving in fertile soils containing plenty of manure and compost. Large leeks require a long growing season so seed is generally sown in pots or in a seedbed from early spring, for planting out in early summer in individual holes, but you can sow seed straight into the ground for harvesting small young leeks. You should be able to harvest leeks from late fall until late spring unless winters are exceptionally hard, when the biggest problem is usually how to lift the plants from frozen ground. Unharvested, they produce magnificent flower heads the summer after sowing — as attractive in a bed as many ornamental Allium species. 'Musselburgh' is a good old-fashioned country-garden variety.

Allium sativum
GARLIC

Height 20 in./45 cm

Wild garlic may have featured as a groundcover in early country gardens, and early gardeners considered garlic a magic plant to ward off witches and ill luck. But the bulbs were not used much as vegetables or seasoning until the mid-20th century. It is an invaluable plant, since it not only provides food, but also secretions from its roots keep diseases away from roses and other herbaceous plants, and garlic seems to improve the health of plants grown nearby. Its scent deters carrot flies, so plant it near carrots in the vegetable plot. For the largest bulbs, plant cloves of garlic 2 inches (5 cm) deep in well-drained fertile soil in the fall for early summer cropping if you have ground prepared; otherwise, plant in spring for a later crop. Surround the slower-growing, tall, thin, garlic leaves with lettuces and other salads for maximum production.

Apium graveolens
CELERY/CELERIAC

Height 24 in./60 cm

Celery is worth growing for the glorious scent of the earthy crop, as well as the flavor. Old-fashioned gardeners used to mound earth, bracken, or sacking around celery plants to blanch the stems; nowadays you can choose a self-blanching variety such as 'Golden Self Blanching'. Sow seeds indoors for planting out 12 inches (30 cm) apart in rich, moisture-retentive, manured soil in sun or partial shade when danger of frost has passed, for harvest in early fall. Celeriac is grown in the same way, harvested before winter frost, then stored in as cool, dry, and dark a place as possible where it should keep for several months.

Asparagus officinalis
ASPARAGUS

Height 6 ft/2 m

Although asparagus has historically been grown in its own special bed, you can grow it in any rich, moist, well-manured soil, where it may be productive for up to 20 years. Try placing it near permanent small fruit bushes that like rich soil. Buy young "crowns" in early spring from a specialized supplier; plant in totally weed-free soil 18 inches (45 cm) apart; and don't harvest the spears until the second year after planting. Cut down foliage when it turns yellow in the fall and mulch well with compost and manure.

Beta vulgaris
BEETS

Height 8-12 in./20-30 cm

Beets have been grown for centuries; the roots can be round, flat, or long, usually with a deep reddish-purple flesh. Their dark reddish green leaves are also edible, cooked like spinach, or eaten young in salads. A rich, light soil is best for beets; they don't like freshly manured ground, but a semi-shady position is fine as long as they get some sun. Sow them in mid- to late spring for summer eating, or in early summer for beets that can be stored in a cool place for winter eating. Don't sow spring beets until the ground is warm or they are likely to bolt without making good-sized roots.

Beta vulgaris
CHARD

Height 12-24 in./30-60 cm

Chard is beautiful, its generous glossy leaves available in brilliant-colored varieties as well as traditional medium green with white stems and ribs. 'Bright Lights' produces leaves in shades of red, purple, yellow, green, and even pink and white striped, with colored ribs; and 'Ruby Chard' is a rich ruby red, though this variety tends to bolt in dry summers. Chard is easy to grow and succeeds under almost any conditions, though crops are lushest on heavily manured soil. It also makes a highly decorative addition to a flowerbed. Sow seeds in spring after frost, thin plants to about 8 inches (20 cm) apart, eating the thinnings; then keep harvesting the plants all year until they die back in winter — the more you pick, the better the plants respond. Plants often regenerate in spring to provide tasty leaves until the next year's plants are ready, but the colored forms are less exuberant the second time around.

Brassica napus
RUTABAGAS
Height 10-15 in./25-36 cm
Once a staple for man and beast, rutabagas are rarely grown in gardens these days, but they are an ideal root for cool, moist conditions. Sow seeds in early summer into fertile soils and roots will be ready for use in early fall, but they can be left in the ground for several months. They are delicious simply boiled and mashed with butter, or in stews.

Brassica oleracea var. acephela
KALE
Height and Spread 24-36 in./60-90 cm
Kale is a strong-tasting leafy vegetable, producing a profusion of leaves through winter and delicate young shoots in spring when there's not much variety in the garden. Sow seeds in late spring to early summer in a seedbed for transplanting into their final growing position in late summer. Kale thrives in rich, well-drained soil, but will cope with poorer conditions than most brassicas. Kales have striking, curly, dark green leaves and make attractive bed plants, particularly if you don't have a vegetable plot. 'Winterbor' is an old variety with very tender, deeply ruffled, gray-green leaves. 'Red Russian' has red-tinged and veined leaves that taste slightly hot. 'Lacinato' is an exceptionally attractive form with sheaves of very slim, dark green, crinkled leaves with creamy-white stems and veins.

Brassica oleracea var. botrytis
CAULIFLOWER
Height 24-36 in./60-90 cm
Cauliflowers are not the easiest of vegetables to grow. They may stubbornly refuse to produce the desired large tight heads if they are checked by a lack of water or nutrients in the soil, or if they are subjected to an unexpected hot or cold spell, which will result in tiny, loose, premature heads. Sow them from spring to summer in very fertile soil, depending whether you're growing tender winter-heading varieties or hardier spring-heading cauliflowers. To protect them

from frost or hot sun, you can wrap the outer leaves around the developing heads. The best choice for a sheltered country garden is the brilliantly white old-fashioned variety 'Snow Crown' or the early spring-cropping purple variety 'Violet Queen', which turns green on cooking and has an excellent flavor.

Brassica oleracea var. capitata
CABBAGES
Height 24 in./60 cm
No traditional country garden was without cabbages, once known as worts, which thrived on manure-rich soil in sun or partial shade and provided food during the lean winter months. There are varieties for summer, fall, and winter cropping, which can be sown throughout the growing season. Summer and fall varieties include red cabbages, along with crinkly leaved Savoy winter cabbages. Spring cabbages often have conical-shaped heads. They are the most troublesome to grow because they can be easily killed in severe winters or bolt without heading up in spring if the weather is too mild and damp.

The earliest varieties of brassicas can be sown into seedbeds as soon as frost is past, then transplanted to their final positions in early summer, or sow seeds indoors and plant seedlings out 18 inches (45 cm) apart. Pick off cabbage caterpillars, or plant hyssop nearby, which seems to keep cabbage butterflies away while attracting lots of helpful insects. Hang sticky yellow traps above rows of cabbages to trap fleabeetle, which can be a dreadful pest to brassicas, or cover rows with floating row cover.

Brassica oleracea var. gemnifera
BRUSSELS SPROUTS
Height 24 in./60 cm
A favorite winter crop, sprouts are worth growing if you have a vegetable plot. They need well-drained, moisture-retentive, but not recently manured soil. Give them firm ground so the top-heavy plants don't fall over. Sow seeds into a prepared seedbed in mid-spring and put plants out into their final places in early summer. Grow as cabbages — see above.

Beta vulgaris — chard, with brassicas, cabbage, and sprouts

Brassicas: cauliflower, Romanesco broccoli, and calabrese

Brassica oleracea var. gongyloides
KOHLRABI
Height 15-24 in./40-60 cm
Very underrated, swollen-stemmed kohlrabi was first grown in German country gardens and in Eastern Europe over 400 years ago, but was never popular in England or France. It prefers light, fertile soil with plenty of moisture, and since it is quick growing, several sowings can be made from early spring to midsummer to get a continuous supply until winter. The swollen stems look rather like turnips and are delicious eaten as a hot vegetable or grated raw in salads. 'White Vienna', 'Green Vienna', and 'Purple Vienna' are good old varieties best harvested young, before the stems get much bigger than tennis balls. If you can get seed for 'Gigante', let it swell to form balls around 9 pounds (4 kg) in weight, which will still be creamy sweet and tender, excellent as a vegetable or in stews.

Brassica oleracea var. Italia
BROCCOLI, CALABRESE
Height 30 in./75 cm
Sprouting broccoli is an excellent hardy cool-garden biennial, producing masses of flowering sprouts for an early spring vegetable. In mild climates sow seed into rich soil in late spring to harvest early the following year, when plants produce the tasty sprouting heads for many weeks. The purple-flowered varieties are hardy in most situations and will overwinter unless the weather is really severe, but the white ones need a more sheltered spot. Calabrese, or green sprouting broccoli varieties, are smaller and faster growing than sprouting varieties, but are not so hardy. Sow them from spring to early summer for harvesting two to three months later. The pale green spiraling heads of Romanesco broccoli are particularly attractive newcomers to a country garden. Grow all brassicas as cabbages. (See page 111.)

Brassica rapa
TURNIPS
Height 10-15 in./25-36 cm
Turnips thrive in cool, moist conditions in soil containing plenty of manure and compost. Sow seed from early spring for summer-harvesting types that need cool weather and bolt in hot, dry conditions; sow winter types in late summer and leave the roots in the ground until hard frosts set in. Summer turnips are small and delicately flavored, tender and delicious as a vegetable, while winter turnips, old country-garden staples, are larger and best used in soups and stews.

Capsicum annuum
BELL AND HOT PEPPERS
Height 24 in./60 cm
Scarcely traditional country-garden plants, but if they had been around sooner, you can be sure country gardeners would have been tempted by their glossy foliage and shining fruits. Sow seed under cover in spring and plant out into light but fertile and moisture-retentive soil in sunny beds when days are warm and the sun is high in the sky — peppers need heat and sunlight. They are also good in tubs and windowboxes. You can't grow very hot peppers outdoors in northern areas, but sweet peppers do well in a warm year and taste much better than the offerings you can find at the supermarket.

Cichorium spp.
ENDIVE
Height 6 in./15 cm, Spread 12 in./30 cm
Traditional country gardeners might think endive is a bit fancy since it is slightly more fuss to grow than most other winter vegetables. It is worth growing the old variety 'Witloof' for an unusual tasty green vegetable, which was popular on the European continent for centuries. Sow in summer into any well-tended garden soil, and either pick and use as slightly bitter salad leaves, or lift the roots and tightly curled young plants in the fall and force them in a box full of compost in the dark, producing delicate tender shoots over winter and into early spring. Don't be tempted to peek too soon; they fare best left entirely in the dark for a couple of months. Just moisten the planting medium every week or two.

Cucurbita spp.
CUCUMBER
Trails or climbs to 9 ft/3 m
Hardly a traditional country garden plant, cucumbers are nonetheless a tasty addition to the vegetable plot. Most can be tricky to grow, but the open-pollinated 'Marketmore' and specialty 'Lemon' cucumbers are easy to grow and produce high, if somewhat late, yields of tasty fruit. Thrives on almost total neglect in sun or partial shade, producing dozens of small fruits in late summer. Sow seeds indoors in pots in spring to plant out in early summer, or sow direct into warm fertile ground in early summer. Keep well watered.

Cucurbita spp.
ZUCCHINI, SUMMER SQUASH
Height and Spread vary
Manure-laden soil and a sunny position is perfect for the greedy squash family, whose sprawling plants can cover several yards, while bush varieties grow to at least 3 feet (90 cm) in height and spread. They were traditionally grown straight onto a manure heap or compost pile. Sow seeds indoors in pots in early spring to plant out two or three weeks after the danger of frost has passed, or sow directly into the ground in early summer, watering well in dry weather until seedlings are growing strongly, and again when fruits are forming. Pick off lower leaves if they show mildew in damp years. Golden zucchini form brilliant yellow fruits on compact bushes, or go for larger varieties, popularly used by country gardeners as winter storage vegetables and for jelly making.

Cynara scolymus
GLOBE ARTICHOKES
Height and Spread 4 ft/1.2 m
Either grow perennial artichokes in the vegetable plot or in beds; they make statuesque plants with their long, silver-gray, toothed leaves and the attractive flowerheads, which are eaten immature or left to open into giant purple thistlelike flowers, very attractive to bees and cut for dried flower arrangements. It is best to

propagate new plants from rooted suckers taken from parent plants in spring; otherwise, sow seed into pots or straight into the ground when it has warmed up in spring. Cut plants back to the ground after harvesting or flowering.

Daucus carota
CARROTS
Height 12-15 in./20-36 cm

Long, tapering, orange carrots are relatively recent compared to stumpy varieties such as 'Parabel' and 'Oxheart'. Carrots are easy to grow in light soil: sow seeds after frost has passed, then thin seedlings when about 4 inches (10 cm) tall. It is a good idea to plant chives or onions nearby to repel carrot fly, which hunt by scent. If your soil is very rich or heavy, don't bother with carrots, but grow other roots such as parsnips.

Foeniculum vulgare var. *dulce*
FENNEL
Height 12-36 in./30-90 cm

The swollen bulb vegetable version of the fennel commonly grown in flowerbeds and herb gardens for its feathery foliage and seeds, bulb

Cynara scolymus

fennel is a relatively recent Italian import, delicious steamed or in salads. Equally as attractive as its seedbearing cousin, it makes an attractive bed plant in a sunny position in rich soil, as well as in the vegetable plot. Sow seeds in midsummer, thinning seedlings to 8 inches (20 cm) apart to give bulbs the chance to swell; keep them well watered, and harvest in the early fall.

Helianthus tuberosus
JERUSALEM ARTICHOKES
Height 10 ft/3 m

Closely related to sunflowers, perennial artichokes are propagated from pieces of tuber planted any time from winter until late spring. Take care when planting them in a small plot — every piece of tuber left in the soil after harvesting will resprout. However, the nutty tubers are delicious, and plants can also make a quick-growing windbreak or screen. They thrive in almost any soil, and although they prefer sun, they will do well in partial shade. The old variety 'Fuseau' is almost knob-free so is the easiest to prepare, and 'Patate' produces large rounded and fairly smooth tubers.

Lactuca sativa
LETTUCES
Height 6-18 in./15-45 cm

Traditional country gardeners would not have cultivated many summer salad vegetables, but salads are an essential part of any vegetable plot. They are tasty, versatile, and fast-growing, filling gaps between other slower-maturing vegetables in cool climates. Plant a mixture of headed varieties and loose-leaved or "cut-and-come-again" or 'Salad Bowl' variety lettuces, which are particularly productive where space is limited, since they can be cut for many weeks before you need to re-sow. They are also ideal for windowboxes and tubs. With careful choice and successional sowing, you can enjoy lettuce from your garden almost all year round in mild climates. The chief problem with growing lettuces is usually slugs which adore the juicy young seedlings, so protect young salads with cloches, traps, and copper barriers.

Lycopersicon esculentum
TOMATOES
Height 12-48 in./30-120 cm

It's worth growing a few tomatoes outdoors even in northern areas, although they are frost tender and need long summers to flourish, but if you have a greenhouse you can choose from a vast number of varieties. These range from standard round red varieties to old-fashioned yellow or white, large black or brownish fruits, pinkish purple balls, oval and plum-shaped fruits. They vary in size from tiny cherry tomatoes to huge beefsteak varieties — the round red globes we know are fairly recent introductions.

Sow seeds indoors in a warm place in early spring, and don't plant out until early summer, hardening them off for a few days beforehand by taking trays of seedlings outdoors during the day and in at night. Plant into a fertile, moisture-retentive soil with plenty of organic matter, and water well. Bush varieties do not need staking; others should be tied to stakes, and suckers pinched out to produce more fruit. All tomatoes are sweetest when they benefit from a long, hot summer, but many varieties will produce a tasty crop in even cool areas if sheltered.

Foeniculum vulgare var dulce

Pastinaca sativa
PARSNIPS

Height 12-15 in./20-36 cm

Parsnips were a staple crop in Europe in the Middle Ages, but lost popularity in most countries except Britain, where they have always remained popular. They thrive in most conditions, although they will split into forked roots if the soil has been too recently manured. The longest-rooted types do best on lighter soils. Seeds are slow to germinate, so avoid sowing them until the soil is thoroughly warm in late spring, for harvesting in the fall and winter. They are extremely hardy vegetables, and most people think they taste best after they have been frosted; they can stay in the ground happily all winter. 'Lancer' is a very sweet, high germinating variety that is an improved type of the old-fashioned 'Harris Model' parsnip.

Phaseolus spp.
POLE BEANS

Height 6–10 ft/2–3 m

No country garden should be without a wigwam of pole beans. Grow old-fashioned 'Scarlet Runner' red-flowered plants as decoration as well as food, perhaps with morning glories (*Convolvulus ipomoea*) growing through them for added drama. Erect a wigwam or triangular frame of stakes or poles in full sun or partial shade, and sow two seeds per hole, 1 inch (2.5 cm) deep after the last frost. Keep plants well watered as flowers and beans appear, and pick beans regularly to encourage more. Green beans won't germinate if the temperatures are too warm; in hot climates grow French beans *(Phaseolus coccineus)* or beans for drying.

Phaseolus vulgaris
BUSH BEANS

Height 15-36 in./38-90 cm

Bush beans are popular in every vegetable patch, as they are easy to grow, mature early, and most varieties are highly productive. As the name implies, they don't need staking, unlike pole beans, which make better use of space but are later maturing. Bush beans will grow in any well-drained garden soil as long as they aren't planted out until the soil is warmed and all danger of frost is long past. One of the tastiest for drying and baking, 'Jacob's Cattle', is a beautiful maroon and white heirloom variety that has been grown for centuries and is particularly good in New England and the North where seasons are short. In small gardens, try another old variety, 'Midnight Black Turtle', which produces lots of pink flowers rather than the more usual white and is good fresh or dried. Bush beans are known as French beans in Europe where they are eaten fresh, sliced in the pod, and rarely used dried.

Pisum sativum var. *sativum*
PEAS

Height 1 1/2–6 ft/45 cm-2 m

Peas were among the earliest vegetables to be cultivated, but early country gardeners would probably have grown them for drying, to be used later in soups and dishes such as pease pudding. Podding peas were established by the 17th century, and many of the taller peas grown today are descendants of these early varieties.

Pastinaca sativa

Phaseolus coccineus

Scorzonera hispanica

Tall varieties are the more traditional country plants; they tend to be prolific and crop over a long period, but need to be well supported. Short varieties crop less well, but are easy to grow. You can sow peas successively from early spring until late summer, for continuous harvest until well into the fall.

Raphanus sativus
RADISHES
Height 6-8 in./15-25 cm
Not just children's salad vegetables, radishes have been grown for thousands of years, and these hot, tasty, little roots are worth growing to fill up bare spaces in summer — fast-growing varieties can provide crops within two to three weeks. They need plenty of moisture and must be thinned soon after sowing — they don't develop properly if overcrowded. They bolt quickly or turn woody if the weather is too hot and they don't get enough water.

Scorzonera hispanica
SCORZONERA
Height 18 in./45 cm
This perennial plant produces long black-skinned but white-fleshed roots that are delicious in the first and second season. This is another vegetable that fell out of popularity centuries ago, but it has delicious flavor and is easy to grow in any fertile soil provided that the ground is not waterlogged.

Solanum melongena
EGGPLANT
Height and Spread 18-24 in./45-60 cm
In a cool garden you may need to grow eggplants under cover, but in a warm, sunny climate you can get a good crop in the vegetable plot or in containers outside. They're not traditional country-garden plants, although they were very widely grown in southern Europe as early as the 8th or 9th century. Seeds should be sown in spring indoors in a warm place and planted out in a greenhouse or polytunnel if possible, or grow them indoors in pots for a while and plant out in summer. They are rather

floppy plants, so stake them well, and keep the soil moist but never waterlogged. They're very attractive plants, with felty, spreading, green leaves and drooping, dusty purple flowers. 'Early Long Purple' has long, deep purple fruit, sometimes mottled with paler purple. 'Violetta di Firenze' has round purple fruits with a pale blush at the stalk end. Both will produce fairly prolifically outdoors in cooler climates; other varieties really need heat to flourish.

Solanum tuberosum
POTATOES
Height 18-24 in./45-60 cm
Traditionally, no country garden would have been without a sizable plot of potatoes. Although they do take up quite a bit of space, do try to grow at least a few rows of potatoes. There's nothing like digging your own and eating them within hours of harvesting. Potatoes are no trouble to grow; they just need a fertile, well-manured soil and plenty of moisture. Purchase seed potatoes in winter and sprout them in a cool light place to get them ready for planting in early spring. Push mounds of earth or rich mulch around the rows as they grow to prevent greening of any tubers near the surface. There are numerous good varieties of early and maincrop potatoes, for mashing, baking, frying, and for salads, but choose blight-resistant varieties. If blight does strike — the virus affects tomatoes, too — you have to destroy your whole crop.

Spinacia oleracea
SPINACH
Height 6-12 in./15-30 cm
Spinach is a fast-growing annual that provides delicious leafy greens from early summer until fall in moist fertile soil in a cool climate, but it doesn't like heat and bolts if the summer is too hot or conditions too dry. Sow seed in early spring and don't let the ground get too dry. One of the tastiest varieties is the very deep-green heavy cropping 'Bloomsdale'. The perennial New Zealand spinach (Tetragonia expansa) is a sprawling plant with milder flavor than annual spinach. It tolerates drought.

Tragopogon porrifolius
SALSIFY
Height 36 in./90 cm
Salsify is rarely grown today—more's the pity because it produces not only tasty roots but also some of the most attractive flowers any plant can boast. Its beautiful purple-blue flowers are so delicately veined with gold they look as though an artist has individually brushed each one. To make them even more exotic, the lovely flowers open for only a few short hours each morning. Some people eat the flower buds, but this seems almost sacrilegous. Salsify is biennial. Sow the seed in spring into deep but light fertile soil to harvest roots from fall through to the following spring. Cook the roots scrubbed but unpeeled; squeeze the skin off after boiling or baking. The flavor is creamy.

Vicia faba
FAVA BEANS
Height 18-40 in./45-100 cm
Originally grown as a staple crop in European fields rather than allowed into gardens, stake plants with twiggy sticks for a traditional look. For an early summer crop, sow seeds outdoors in a sunny spot in late fall in fertile soil. Otherwise, start seeds in pots indoors in early spring and plant seedlings out 6-10 inches (15-25 cm) apart in early summer to be harvested 3-4 months later. 'Winsor' is a reliable variety. Fava beans don't do well in hot climates.

Zea mays
CORN
Height 6 ft/2 m
Corn is only half hardy and not reliable in cooler gardens, unless you choose a northern cultivar. Even if you only get a few ripe cobs, it's worth it for the taste of freshly picked and cooked corn, which deteriorates quickly after picking. Sow into warm soil — corn won't germinate at soil temperatures below 50°F (10°C). It needs a long frost-free growing season, taking from 70-120 days from sowing to harvesting.

Small fruit

If you possibly can, grow some small fruit even if space is limited. There's nothing quite like a bowl of freshly picked, sun-kissed strawberries or grapes straight from the garden, or sweetly perfumed raspberries. There are space-saving ways of growing most fruit: bushes can be grown as cordons or fans on a cool wall; some varieties of raspberries grow in a neat bush; blackberries and their relatives can be grown as part of a hedge or trained neatly along fences; and strawberries can be dotted in beds or grown in a pot or hanging basket.

Fragaria spp.
STRAWBERRIES
Height 12 in./30 cm, Spread 12 in./30 cm

Wild strawberries were undoubtedly brought into European cottage gardens from woodlands very early, and these small alpine varieties (*Fragaria vesca semperflorens*) are wonderful in country gardens, edging paths and producing their small, dark, red, slightly scented fruits over the whole of the summer in semi-shade as well as sun, content to peer out from under the foliage of other plants. Plant them from seed in spring, and they will spread swiftly from runners. The large-fruited types were native in North America and became popular country-garden fruits. Plant small plants in spring or summer, depending whether they're summer- or autumn-fruiting varieties, 2 feet (60 cm) apart in fertile well-drained soil. Strawberries thrive in a slightly acid soil, so mulch if possible with leaf mold or compost including pine needles. Water growing plants well, and when the fruit starts to color, mulch with straw underneath to keep the berries off the ground and away from slugs. After fruiting, cut back the foliage to just above the crown of new leaves in the center of the plant. To propagate, root a few of the small plants that grow on the ends of the runners. 'Sparkle' is a reliable summer variety; 'Tristar' produces delicious berries from late summer well into the fall. Strawberries are very happy growing in well-watered medium with their roots restricted in pots; you can move the container into a sunny spot and also keep your fruits out of slugs' way. Small-fruited varieties will crop well over many weeks when they are grown in hanging baskets.

Rheum rhubarbarum
RHUBARB
Height 2-3 ft/60-90 cm, Spread 3 ft/90 cm

Ideal for a shady, moist spot in the yard where sun-loving fruit or vegetables won't grow, rhubarb plants are very decorative with their bright pink-red shoots unfurling in early spring into stiff, dark red stalks and architectural leaves. 'Ace of Hearts' and 'Bowles Crimson' are good reliable varieties. In late winter cover the root with a large bucket, clay pot, or traditional terracotta rhubarb forcing pot, and remove it in early spring. If you wish, propagate plants by dividing the crowns after harvesting, but few yards ever need more than one clump of rhubarb.

Ribes nigrum
BLACKCURRANTS
Height and Spread 3-4 ft/90-120 cm

Blackcurrants can be grown as bushes, traditionally in a row at the end of the vegetable garden, or fan- or cordon-trained against a north or east wall. Very hardy and prolific even in cold gardens, they prefer a sunny position and need rich, deep, well-manured soil. Cut plants back to within 2 inches (5 cm) of the ground to encourage new shoots when you plant blackcurrant bushes. Blackcurrants fruit on new shoots off older wood, so you can prune them hard in winter once they are established, cutting out all old wood to keep the centers of the plants open and growth vigorous, and cutting the whole plant back as hard as you want to. Mulch currant bushes well with manure in winter. The varieties 'Malvern Cross' and 'Black Consort' both produce a good crop of large, succulent berries.

Ribes rubrum
WHITECURRANTS AND REDCURRANTS
Height and Spread 3-4 ft/90-120 cm

Like blackcurrants, these can be grown beside north- or east-facing walls. The big difference between the currants is that red and white currants fruit on one-year-old wood, so you must be a bit more careful when pruning them. Don't cut them back to the ground when you plant them in spring, fall, or early winter, depending on your climate; cut out fruited shoots after cropping, and prune back to the current year's shoots in late fall. 'Versailles' has very round creamy white fruit; 'Wilder' has high yields of large fruit.

Ribes uva-crispa
GOOSEBERRIES
Height and Spread 3-4 ft/90-120 cm

The first bushes to fruit, gooseberries were grown in European country gardens as long ago as the 16th century. By the 19th century there were dozens of local varieties. They are often grown at one end of a row of currants. If you're short of space, try growing a standard gooseberry on a 2-3 foot (60-90 cm) stem, which can be underplanted with bulbs, salads, or flowers. Gooseberries prefer fairly rich, well-manured soil and a sunny position, but they're tough and will survive most conditions except extreme damp since they can be rather susceptible to mildew. Very prickly, fortunately the only pruning gooseberries need is clipping in late fall or winter depending on your climate, or after fruiting to maintain their shape, and it's a good idea to mulch bushes with manure each winter. 'Welcome' is a good cooking variety and berries ripen to sweet dessert fruits. 'Pixwell' is nearly thornless.

Rubus spp.
BLACKBERRIES, LOGANBERRIES, TAYBERRIES
Height and Spread vary

If you garden in the country, don't bother to grow blackberries. Garden varieties rarely taste as good as the wild ones that grow prolifically in so many areas and make an excellent addition to a mixed country hedge. Otherwise train cultivated varieties on wires along a fence. Cut a newly planted blackberry bush right down to the ground in the fall and train the next year's new shoots along horizontal wires. After they fruit, cut the fruited shoots right out and keep training new shoots, cutting them out each year after fruiting. Blackberries aren't fussy about position, but all cultivated fruits crop best if they are given rich, fertile soil and plenty of moisture, and ripen into the sweetest berries in full sun. 'Oregon Thornless' is a good garden variety, the best for training on wires.

Loganberries, tayberries, boysenberries, and other hybrid berries are crosses from raspberries and blackberries. Much neater than blackberries, they have large, succulent berries, sometimes slightly sour to taste, and are suitable for eating either raw or cooked. Grow them in a sunny position, trained up wires and planted in rich soil. Prune them in the same way as blackberries by cutting back fruited shoots after harvesting and then training new shoots into the framework of wires. 'L654' is the only named loganberry. It has very succulent, large, dark fruits, and no thorns. Boysenberries and smaller tayberries are also thornless.

Rubus idaeus
RASPBERRIES
Height and Spread vary

Summer-fruiting raspberries take up more space than fall-fruiting varieties, which make a neat bush (height 4 ft/1.2 m, spread 3 ft/1 m) that can be chopped back to within about 3 inches (8 cm) of the ground after fruiting, so choose according to the size of your garden. Plant fall varieties in spring, and summer varieties in the fall in sunny positions into well-manured, moist ground. Train summer-fruiting varieties on posts and wires. (See page 40.)

Vitis vinifera
GRAPE VINES
Height and Spread vary

Grapes were much more commonly grown in even cool gardens several hundred years ago, and they are worth trying if you have the space. A vine-covered arbor is lovely from early summer — when the young shoots curl and twine around supports — into fall, with its bunches of fruit and attractive reddening leaves. Purely ornamental varieties are a great bonus to a garden, and you can easily get good edible or wine grapes if you have a cool greenhouse. But if you want to try productive outdoor vines, check with your Cooperative Extension Service or local nurseries to learn which cultivars will fruit in your area.

You need to prune and train vines to encourage them to fruit, but it's not a complicated procedure. Plant vines into rich, fertile, moisture-retentive soil 5 feet (1.5 m) apart, on posts and three wires, the top one about 4 feet (1.2 m) tall, and cut plants back to within three buds from the ground. In the first year, allow three shoots to grow and train them vertically. The following spring, pull two branches down and tie them to the lowest wire, pruning the third back to three buds to provide the shoots for the following year. The horizontal branches will produce the fruiting shoots, which should be allowed to grow vertically. When they reach the top wire, pinch out the tops. Cut out the spent shoots and keep training by tying-in two vertical shoots and cutting a third back to three buds. However, if your vines won't produce much fruit despite your best efforts, don't hesitate to take them out and use the garden space for something more productive or decorative.

Rhubarb

Blackcurrants

Gooseberries

Raspberries

Tree fruit

Lucky country gardeners will inherit a plot with a mature apple tree or two, or perhaps a variety of fruit trees. If these have been neglected, you may be able to bring them back into a productive state with careful pruning. It's best to consult a specialist rather than tackling a very old overgrown tree yourself. Try to preserve old trees; they may be traditional varieties that flourish in your particular situation. There are thousands of varieties of apple trees in particular, many specially developed to suit a particular local range of soil and climate conditions. Even if they are common varieties, remember that it will take about 15 years for a newly planted tree to grow into a mature shade-producing specimen, and there's nothing like a mature tree for setting the stage of a garden. If you're starting afresh and have a reasonable-sized plot, plan for a small orchard of mixed apple, pear, and plum trees. If you have room for only one free-standing tree, make it an apple — there's little that evokes a country garden more. And don't think of fruit trees just in terms of their productivity; their beautiful white or pink and white blossoms are one of the glories of a spring garden.

There is space in even a tiny yard to grow fruit against walls and fences; or if your plot is surrounded by a hedge, train a tree or two on mounted post-and-wire supports. Fans are a lovely shape for country gardens, providing trees with maximum warmth from a south- or west-facing wall, and are 'the best way to grow slightly tender fruit such as apricots, peaches, nectarines, and figs. Also, close pruning increases the amount of fruiting wood within easy reach and is a highly productive method of growing fruit. Plums, cherries, apples, and pears also make good fan-trained trees. Espaliers are another attractive, productive shape, best for apples and pears, and cordons are very space-efficient. Step-over fruit trees are the most compact of all, giving productive edging to a vegetable bed — trained as single-tier espaliers, they take an area only 1 foot (30 cm) tall.

Cultivation

All fruit trees should be planted in generous holes back-filled with plenty of well-aged manure or compost and a handful of bonemeal. Firm trees in well by treading the ground around them with your heel and attach them to a short 2 foot (60 cm) stake for their first years. Soil should be moisture-retentive, and trees should be kept well-watered, particularly during the first vital years while they are getting established and when fruit is swelling, but they don't like heavy soil that gets waterlogged. If you remove an old fruit tree, don't plant another one in the same place unless you have thoroughly dug up a large area and completely refreshed the soil with masses of aged manure and compost.

Problem solving

Fruit trees can be host to a wide variety of pests. One simple way to alleviate pest problems is to encourage birds onto fruit trees over winter by hanging suet balls on branches. The birds will then move on to seek out and eat overwintering grubs of insects such as codling moths that hide in cracks in the bark. Sticky tanglefoot-covered bands around the trunks prevent crawling insects, particularly ants, from colonizing the trees — ants protect aphids that can be a particular nuisance on apple trees. Remove aphids by washing or hosing them off with water, and by planting nasturtiums to twine around trunks, or underplanting trees with scented herbs such as lavender or hyssop that encourage beneficial insects that prey on aphids. Scare birds off trees by hanging shiny items such as foil disks or CDs in the trees and by covering them with netting.

You shouldn't have disease problems if trees are planted in the right conditions and you practice good maintenance: when you prune a tree, make sure you use sharp pruning knives and saws to make clean angled cuts, and don't leave debris lying around.

Few of us are fortunate to have sufficient space for the traditional small orchard once typical of rural gardens. However, fruit trees are a valuable part of every country garden, in any situation, and can be grown trained flat against boundaries where space is limited.

PRUNING

■ You can train your own trees (see page 43), but it's easy to buy ready-trained trees. Pruning trained shapes is not difficult.

■ Apples and pears are pruned after they have fruited: prune shoots that come straight from the main branches back to about 3 inches (8 cm), always cutting just above a bud, and cutting any side shoots coming out of these stems back to 1 inch (2.5 cm).

■ Peaches and nectarines fruit on wood made the year before, so in winter cut out all shoots that have fruited the previous year and tie in a replacement shoot, pinching out the tip when the shoot has made five leaves. Pinch out all other shoots apart from one on each branch, which must be left to grow as the replacement shoot for the next year.

■ Figs, plums, cherries, and apricots are pruned early in the year as they start to put out spring growth; reduce all overcrowded shoots — all those growing outward from the wall and those not needed to increase the size of the tree — by cutting them back to two or three buds.

Cydonia oblonga

QUINCES

Height 20 ft/6 m

Hardy quince trees used to be very popular in country gardens because they are so ornamental as well as productive, producing highly-scented, large, soft, creamy white blossoms in spring and fragrant, fuzzy, yellow-green applelike fruits in the fall when the leaves turn a good reddish color before dropping. Fruits are delicious in pies, jams, and jellies. 'Smyrna' is a popular cultivar because of its flavor and fragrance.

Blenheim Orange apples

Ficus carica

FIGS

Height 33 ft/10 m

One of the world's oldest cultivated fruits, figs were taken to Britain by the Romans and to America by the colonists. In addition to bearing delicious fruit in hot summers, they have lovely, shiny, gray bark and stunning, large, rounded, cut leaves with a subtle scent in the sun. In order to get a good crop, you need to restrict the roots of figs, so plant trees into a hole lined with paving slabs or an old trough. They like very rich soil, and gardeners used to plant a slab of meat in the manure-filled hole when they planted figs, but bonemeal will do. 'Brown Turkey' is the ideal outdoor variety, fruiting very well against a west wall or in a south-facing corner of the yard, with 'Brunswick' a close second. Don't water the plants too heavily as the fruits are swelling or they may split, but fig trees do benefit from continuous feeding all summer with a high potash fertilizer or good compost. Some gardeners counsel removing the small fruits that are left unripe on the tree at the end of summer, but it isn't necessary; however, these will fall off rather than developing further the following year unless you have an exceptionally mild winter. In frost-prone yards it is a good idea to protect trees in winter with straw, burlap, or even bubblewrap. In very cold areas, you may want to overwinter the protected tree in an unheated garage or lie it down in a hand-dug depression and bury it for the winter.

Malus spp.

APPLES

Heights vary

Most apples need at least two trees of different varieties to insure pollination and subsequent fruiting, so if you have room for only one tree make sure it is a self-fertile variety. Plant bare-rooted trees in late winter or early spring, stake them firmly, and water very well for the first years. Planting distance depends on the training method you use: cordon trees can be planted 30 inches (75 cm) apart, fans and espaliers about 9 feet (3 m). Don't allow trees to fruit the first year after planting — removing blossoms encourages strong development.

There are literally thousands of varieties of apples, and everyone is guided by different choices. First decide what size and shape of tree you want: if you are training your own trees, choose apples on semi-dwarf M26 rootstock, but if you are growing freestanding trees, MM106 medium-sized rootstock produces stronger trunks. Or choose half standard for all but the largest plot, where you can plant an old-fashioned standard. Then decide whether you want early or late fruiting, early or late flowering, whether you want dessert or cooking apples, instant eating or long storage varieties. Check with neighbors and your extension agent to find out what apples grow well in your area and what pollinators they require. Some varieties are a nightmare to grow without chemicals — their heyday was in Victorian times when an army of under-gardeners kept them in order. Many new cultivars such as 'Redfree', 'Sweet 16,' and 'Liberty' grow well in most of the United States and are resistant to many diseases. 'Granny Smith' is a good choice for zones 6-9 but is not disease resistant.

Mespilus germanica

MEDLARS

Height 16 ft/5 m

Very old and highly ornamental fruit trees, medlars bear beautiful single white flowers in spring. They make a beautiful medium-sized, rounded tree, and the leaves color well in the fall. Interesting fruits like squashed, hairy pears are rather an acquired taste, and need to be "bletted" before use, which means they need to soften off the tree until their skin is wrinkled and the flesh is soft and brown. If you can't face them fresh, medlar jelly is a delicious preserve.

Morus nigra

MULBERRIES

Height 30 ft/10 m

Mulberries were once widely grown, beautiful fruiting shade trees with heart-shaped leaves.

The trees are slow to mature but live productive lives for a century or more, and after 4-5 years they will start to produce delicious fruit similar to loganberries, the harvest increasing as trees age and continuing for many decades. Mulberries need very rich, moist soil in a sunny place and are very thirsty trees, terribly sensitive to lack of water. Young trees die easily from drought. A recent variety, 'Chelsea,' is comparatively compact and has the advantage of fruiting well even as a relatively young tree.

Prunus spp.
CHERRIES
Height 16 ft/5 m
Cherries are beautiful trees in flower and fruit, but if you're going to get any fruit, sweet cherries need a very sunny spot and careful netting, or birds will strip them bare. Although trees are hardy, you may need to throw floating row cover over them to protect blossom and buds from late frosts. 'Stella' and 'Duke' are good varieties, self-fertile and compact. Sour Morello cherries are best of all for a shady yard — their preferred situation is fan-trained against a north wall.

Prunus domestica
PLUMS
Height 16 ft/5 m
Plum trees are among the first to bloom in spring. They need a sheltered site so the pretty white flowers aren't knocked off by spring frost. You also need to make sure you have a supply of early flowering plants in the yard to attract pollinators onto the plum trees so the fruit will set. Traditional gardeners often included wall flowers near fruit trees for this reason. Damsons and bullaces were often grown as hedgerow plants, with other plums in the orchard. Late summer-fruiting and self-fertile 'Victoria' remains a firm favorite, with its red and yellow fruits. 'Methley' ripens in July and grows best in the northwest; 'Mt Royalc' thrives in zones 4 and 5 and ripens in August or September. Wasps can be a nuisance when plums are ripening. Hang traps from branches — jars of sugary water with holes in their foil tops.

Prunus italica
GREENGAGE PLUMS
Height 16 ft/5 m
Soft-skinned summer fruits, greengages are increasingly difficult to buy because they don't handle well, so this is reason enough to try to include this delicious type of plum in your garden. Self-fertile and shade-tolerant 'Oulins Golden Gage' has golden yellow fruit with the classic honeyed taste. 'Cambridge Gage' is pale green and sweet.

Prunus persica
PEACHES
Height 16 ft/5 m
A peach is a beautiful tree for a west- or south-facing wall with pretty pink blossoms and delicious fruit in a good year. Peaches like cold winters and dry springs, and need a long hot summer for fruit to ripen; they won't do well in a cool, damp place. They are susceptible to peach leaf curl, a viral infection spread by rain, which makes leaves spot, brown, curl, and drop; prevent this by growing the tree under a temporary plastic porch, covering the tree from early spring until early summer, or spray with Bordeaux mixture twice as the buds start to swell. In the fall, pick up all old leaves and burn rather than compost them. 'Reliance' and 'Redhaven' are reliable varieties.

Pyrus communis
PEARS
Height 12 ft/3.5 m
Slightly more tender than apples, most pears require a warm sunny garden to flourish, and are particularly happy trained on a west wall. Their dark cut bark is very attractive in winter — you often find old pear trees in walled gardens. The easiest variety to grow is 'Seckel', a small pear with rough skin and wonderful flavor and texture. 'Comice' produces very heavy crops of deliciously sweet, juicy fruit right at the end of the fall, in zones 6-9. 'Maricourt' grows well in the southeast, while 'Ure' grows well in protected spots as far north as zones 3 and 4.

Medlar

Peaches

Comice pears

Hedges

Hedges form a wonderful backdrop to any yard and are particularly good in windy situations since they let some wind filter through, while solid fences can trap wind and create turbulent spots. Your choice will largely depend on space, whether you want an evergreen boundary, a low or high hedge, and how much time you have for maintenance — privet hedges are traditional, low, country-garden hedges but need regular clipping, while yew or holly need only an annual pruning to keep vigor and shape, and mixed hedging needs only a light trimming to keep it under control.

A boundary of mixed native hedging plants is a wonderful border for a rural garden, but you need to allow at least 4 feet 6 inches (1.25 m) spread. Among the beauties of mixed hedging are the range of colors, textures, blossoms, and fruits from fast-maturing blackthorn (sloe), hawthorn, field maple, hazel, and crabapple, perhaps interwoven with honeysuckle, dog rose, blackberry, and wild clematis *(Clematis viticella)*. It will also provide a haven for wildlife; wildflowers will thrive beneath it, and it will be impenetrable.

Beech hedges have particularly attractive pale spring growth, though some people don't care for their rusty brown winter covering, and they are slow to get going. Privet is easy to establish and maintain, but if you want a reliable evergreen hedge, yew is the quality choice and can be clipped into arches and all sorts of fanciful shapes. Reputedly slow growing, in fact, if it is planted into well-manured trenches and fed heavily for the first years, it dashes away and only needs clipping once annually. Holly is a wonderful hedging material, on its own or mixed, and berberis and pyracantha make impenetrable flowering hedges with attractive berries in fall.

Watch out for hedging plants marketed as "fast-growing." Leylandii conifers were for years recommended as an almost instant evergreen boundary, but they continue to grow to form towering dark trees that too soon become more of a menace than a pleasure. Plant Leylandii in a country garden only if you are prepared to trim it very regularly to keep it as a low clipped hedge; otherwise, avoid it.

For a touch of formality, find space for a low, box-hedged miniature knot garden, and fill it with herbs or geraniums and something upright like these miniature standard roses.

PLANTING HEDGES

Plant bare-rooted or container-grown hedging plants into a trench at least 2 feet (60 cm) wide and 18 inches (45 cm) deep, with a thick layer of compost and manure in the base. Hedges of berberis, escallonia, pyracantha, and holly should be planted 18 inches (45 cm) apart in a single row. Hornbeam, beech, privet, hawthorn, and mixed deciduous hedges should be planted in two staggered rows 12-18 inches (30-45 cm) apart to establish a solid hedge within three years. Yew trees should be planted 18 inches (45 cm) apart into very well-manured soil — don't trim them for the first five or six years or until they reach their required height for clipping. Keep hedges very well-fed and watered as they get established.

PRUNING HEDGES

BEECH late summer

BERBERIS AND PYRACANTHA early summer

ESCALLONIA late summer after flowering

HAWTHORN after flowering

HOLLY late summer

HORNBEAM late summer

MIXED NATIVE HEDGING summer after nesting birds have reared their young

PRIVET regularly from spring to fall

YEW late summer

Acer campestre
FIELD MAPLE

This small tree, long planted as part of country-garden hedges and quick to establish itself under most conditions, adapts well to hedging. It has bright red young shoots and leaves, and distinctive orange-yellow fall coloring.

Berberis spp.
BARBERRY

This spiny-stemmed shrub has been cultivated in European gardens for 500 years. Originally, its small berries were pickled, but it is now grown for its colorful foliage, flowers and berries. It grows well in poor soils, makes impenetrable hedges, and tolerates shade and wind. *B. x stenophylla* (height 10 ft/ 3 m) is a vigorous evergreen orange-berried, black-fruited form for hedging. Low-growing *B. darwinii* (height 6 ft 6 in./2 m) has glossy green leaves and produces bright orange flowers all spring, followed by purplish blue oval fruits. Deciduous *B. thunbergii* (height 3 ft/1 m) has bluish green leaves that turn orange and red in fall, with pale yellow flowers in spring followed by brilliant red berries. *B. thunbergii* 'Atropurea Nana' (height 2 ft/60 cm) has small, oval, purple leaves and yellow flowers in spring, followed by scarlet fruits. Cut berberis back hard as you plant it for hedging.

Buxus sempervirens
BOX

This low hedging plant (one of the finest for topiary) has been used at boundaries or to edge beds for centuries. Box is not fussy where you plant it as long as you provide moisture and well-manured soil, and space plants 9 inches (22 cm) apart. *B. microphylla* has very dense, rounded growth and smaller leaves than *B. sempervirens* and has recently become popular because it is somewhat faster growing, but stick with one variety or the other and don't mix the two, because they have different growth habits and *B. microphylla* has a rather different colored leaf. The more vigorous *B. suffruticosa* can be grown to form hedges or topiary features up to 5 feet (1.5 m) tall. Low box hedges are quite high maintenance; they should be clipped regularly between spring and fall to keep them in shape. With taller hedges and topiary features, you can get away with clipping them once annually in early summer.

Carpinus betulus
HORNBEAM

An alternative to beech for those who don't like the rustling brown leaves of beech in winter, hornbeam is faster to get established than beech in cold or exposed situations.

Cornus spp.
DOGWOOD

Vigorous deciduous dogwood is a very good-value hedging plant, as happy in cool, damp situations as in drier, sunnier spots. It produces fine crimson-purple autumn leaves, well-colored winter shoots in shades of red and yellow, clusters of small but attractive white flowers, and black berries. *Cornus sanguinea* is the most common variety for hedges. 'Winter Beauty' has bright orange-yellow and red winter shoots.

Corylus avellana
HAZELNUT

This tree makes a good inclusion in a mixed hedge for its catkins and fruit, both of which appear in greater profusion if the plant is kept well trimmed rather than being allowed to grow tall. The cultivar 'Contorta' is also useful for producing canes to support climbing flowers and vegetables. But be aware that hazelnuts act as a squirrel magnet, and these little creatures can be very destructive in a yard.

Crataegus monogyna
HAWTHORN

This is the traditional hedging plant for cottage gardens, originally grown as an impenetrable

Cornus

Coryllus avellana

barrier to keep livestock out, and it still a wonderful choice. Its white spring flowers are known as May blossom, and many people still consider it unlucky to pick them and bring them into the house. This stems from numerous ancient beliefs and warnings about picking white flowers, and could be because the flowers do actually smell a bit like rotting flesh as they age. Hawthorn hedges establish quickly if you cut plants right back as you plant them. They are happy in most situations.

Escallonia spp.
ESCALLONIA

These evergreen shrubs make attractive hedges up to 6 feet (2 m) tall with prolific masses of slightly scented flowers in early and midsummer. They are particularly useful in rather exposed areas. *Escallonia* 'Donard Seedling' is a vigorous arching form producing masses of saucer-shaped, pink-tinged white flowers opening from pink buds in early summer; 'Apple Blossom' has lovely blooms like apple blossom.

Euonymus europaeus
SPINDLE

Another plant definitely worth considering, spindle makes a very attractive component of a mixed hedge, largely because of its bright pink, quartered fruits in late fall that split open to reveal bright orange seeds.

Fagus sylvatica
BEECH

A lovely hedging plant, beech forms a dense hedge with glorious bright green spring growth, and the autumn leaves will hang on all winter, providing permanent cover. Typical beech hedges are trimmed at anything between 3 feet (1 m) and 15 feet (4.5 m).

Ilex aquifolium
HOLLY

Another ancient tree, holly in hedges is long lasting, attractive, and easy to maintain with an annual pruning. Holly is tolerant of shade and the ideal glowing border to a shady-sided yard,

with red berries as an extra in early winter before the birds get them. When you clip in spring, leave some plants to grow tall, and you'll be able to prune them into a variety of shapes — pyramids and balls rising from a clipped holly hedge look particularly attractive and traditional. The worst thing about holly is weeding beds in front of it after pruning! If you like variegated forms, there are dozens to choose from. Among the most reliable are 'Golden Queen' with leaves edged in creamy-yellow and 'Silver King' with creamy white margins to the leaves, but they are slightly less vigorous than the species.

Ligustrum vulgare
PRIVET

Seen in front of old country gardens everywhere, low, dense, small-leaved, dark green privet hedges were once almost universal and are very attractive. Almost evergreen, they bear trusses of scented white flowers in summer followed by small black berries. They are tolerant of rather thin, poor soils, particularly very stony, chalky limestone soils. Their chief disadvantage is that they need regular trimming from spring to fall, because they get scruffy very quickly.

Prunus institia
BULLACE

Traditionally included in country hedges, this stocky variety of plum produces scented white blossoms in spring, followed by round purple fruits in the fall.

Prunus spinosa
BLACKTHORN, SLOE

A glorious country hedging plant. Use it on its own or as part of a mixed hedge, which should be trimmed annually once it is established, and kept at any height above 4 feet (1.2 m). If you don't trim country hedges frequently but let them grow into trees, you'll eventually have to lay them, which means chopping down the main stems, thinning them, and training them to regrow as a thick low hedge, but strictly speaking, this is more of a rural craft than a

Escallonia 'Apple blossom'

Fagus sylvatica

Prunus spinosa

gardening technique. Blackthorn is one of the earliest plants to bloom, covered in white flowers in mid-spring, and producing round purple berries — sloes — in the fall.

Pyracantha spp.
PYRACANTHA

Spiny evergreen shrubs, they have been popular in country gardens for centuries, both as wall-trained shrubs and very effective hedges 4-6 feet (1.2-2 m) tall, surviving almost any conditions with equanimity. The thorny nature of pyracanthas makes them efficient security hedges. Sometimes also known as firethorn, they are brilliant for wildlife with their dense shrubby cover and huge clusters of berries in the fall following their rather insignificant white blossoms. *P.* 'Mohave' is vigorous and bushy with very long-lasting bright red berries. *P. coccinea* makes very dense growth with masses of bright scarlet berries; *P.* 'Golden Dome' is another densely spreading variety with an abundance of golden-yellow berries.

Rhamnus catharticus
BUCKTHORN

Less popular these days than it deserves, buckthorn forms a dense spiny hedge with dark green leaves that turn yellow in the fall. It has yellow flowers in spring, and round red fruit in fall. These fruit are a popular food crop in parts of Eastern Europe. Buckthorn should be trimmed hard on planting, then pruned after flowering to keep it in shape.

Rosa canina
DOG ROSE

Another good candidate for inclusion in a mixed country hedge. Put a dog rose into a well-manured planting hole to twine through its neighbors, where it will display its pale flowers and red hips.

Taxus baccata
YEW

The king of all hedging plants, yew is easy to establish on all but waterlogged soils if you feed it with plenty of manure and keep it well-watered, mulching it well in summer with grass clippings or aged manure. It has an undeserved reputation for being slow-growing; yews will grow from 18 inch (45 cm) container-grown plants to a solid 8 foot (2.5 m) hedge in seven years or so and will continue happily for well over a hundred years, maybe several hundred. Yew needs to be clipped annually in late summer. It is one of the few conifers that will regrow from old wood if it gets out of hand, so even old uncared-for yew hedges can usually be brought back to life within a few years, and yew is a marvelous tree for topiary.

Viburnum opulus
GUELDER ROSE

This branching shrub makes an insignificant specimen plant but an excellent hedging candidate, growing particularly well in wet places. It is happy to scramble through other plants, producing white flowers in early summer and clusters of glistening, scarlet red berries in the fall, as well as very striking, crimson and yellow fall foliage.

Dog roses flourish in this mixed country hedge.

Shrubs

When you think of country gardens, it is always the herbaceous plants, along with roses and climbers, that first spring to mind. But while these are undoubtedly the main flowering glories of an abundant garden, you will also need a framework of shrubs for permanent height and structure, and a few evergreens to retain interest year-round. There is an enormous range to choose from: the following short list suggests a few starting points, including some shrubs that have been popular with country gardeners for hundreds of years.

Buddleia davidii
BUTTERFLY BUSH
Height 8-10 ft/2.4-3 m, Spread 5 ft/1.5 m
The long cylindrical clusters of scented purple flowers waving at the tips of *Buddleia davidii's* arching stems should be an essential part of every summer country garden. From midsummer on, the bush will be covered with butterflies feasting at their favorite café. Buddleias are sun-loving plants, preferring a warm site, but unfussy about soil. Don't fear that a buddleia will be too large for a small yard — you can chop these vigorous shrubs virtually down to the ground in spring and they will regrow happily, blooming more profusely the more severely they are pruned. White, pink, blue, and purple varieties are available. *B. globosa* is often seen in old country gardens; it forms a spreading semi-evergreen shrub (height and spread 8 ft/2.4 m) and produces dense clusters of spherical orange-yellow flowers in early summer, equally beloved by butterflies. This is one of those plants you either love or hate, so make sure you know which camp you fall in before you plant one! *B. alternifolia* is a wonderful shrub for small yards; particularly long clusters of intensely fragrant flowers hang from arching gray-leaved branches in summer.

Cistus spp.
ROCK ROSE
Height 4 ft/1.2 m, Spread 3 ft/1 m
A lovely free-flowering shrub for the middle of a sunny bed. Large, open-faced, five-petaled flowers with bright yellow stamens are produced over a long period in summer. They prefer well-drained soil and can be short-lived in damp gardens, but they are so pretty it is still worth growing them in any country garden. If they fail in your beds, they will grow happily in containers. *C. purpureus* has dark pink petals with maroon splashes at the base; *C. × cyprius* has white flowers with triangular yellow and crimson marks at the base of the petals; *C. creticus* has purple-pink crinkled flowers with orange stamens. Rather stiff-stemmed, rock roses don't like to be pruned hard, so just prune them lightly after flowering to encourage a bushy habit. Don't let them get leggy because you won't be able to prune them back to shape.

Fuchsia

Daphne mezereum
MEZEREON
Height 3 ft/1 m, Spread 2 ft/60 cm
A real treasure of a plant, sweetly fragrant, pinkish purple flowers cover the stems of this neat bush heralding the arrival of spring. The scent is superb, spreading widely around the late winter garden. Daphnes are less widely grown than they should be, and considered rather temperamental, but they thrive in any chalky, well-drained soil in sun or partial shade as long as they are not disturbed. They aren't generally very long-lived, so take stem cuttings once the plant is established. *Daphne odora marginata* is a similar-sized evergreen shrub with shiny, oval leaves edged with cream and strongly scented, purplish pink and cream flowers through the winter.

Forsythia spectabilis
FORSYTHIA
Height 6 ft/1.8 m, Spread 5 ft/1.5 m
The arching dark green branches of this bush are massed with bright yellow flowers in spring. It's very easy to grow, in sun or partial shade, so its cheerful spring flowers have featured for hundreds of years in country gardens, but it is another of those plants you either love or hate!

Fuchsia spp.
Height and Spread 6 in.-4 ft/15 cm-1.2 m
Unlike the tender annual fuchsias so popular in summer containers, the shrubs are hardy woody plants whose plump pendant buds open into pretty-skirted flowers in summer, often in two colors. Fuchsias need a sunny spot and well-drained soil, and you need to cut back the

shoots and then cover the plants in early winter in colder gardens; otherwise, prune hard in spring. *F.* 'Hidcote Beauty' (12-20 in./30-45 cm) has light green foliage and cream and pink flowers; *F.* 'Marinka' is a low-growing trailing form with dark green leaves with reddish undersides and masses of two-tone red flowers. 'Golden Marinka' has variegated green and yellow leaves. The compact bushy 'Tom Thumb' (height and spread 6-12 in./15-30 cm) produces masses of red and mauve flowers in early summer. 'Mrs Popple' is a vigorous, hardy

old variety (to 4 ft/1.2 m) with masses of red and violet flowers in late summer.

Garrya elliptica
TASSEL BUSH
Height and Spread 10 ft/3 m
The long silver-gray tassels of this evergreen bush are striking throughout winter, and this useful shrub is not fussy about soil. Although it doesn't like cold winds, it grows well against a cold, north-facing wall. It shouldn't need pruning, just light reshaping in spring.

Hydrangea macrophylla
HYDRANGEA
Height and Spread 3-5 ft/1-1.5 m
Old-fashioned hydrangeas divide into two groups, mopheads and lacecaps. Pink varieties will flourish anywhere, but you'll only get good blue flowers on acid soils, although it used to be common practice to place a few old nails in the planting holes, or water with vinegar to encourage the blue shades. They flower most profusely in any good soil in semi-shady sites, but can also put on a good show in full sun, although the flowers won't last so long. Mopheads are typical old country-garden flowers, with their generous round heads of pink or blue flowers through summer into fall. Their heads dry well and make attractive winter flower arrangements. 'Goliath' is a vigorous variety with very large flowerheads; 'Blue Bonnet' has very dense heads of rich blue to pink flowers. Lacecap hydrangeas have flattened flowerheads surrounded by a ring of open blossoms. 'Blue Wave' has blue centers surrounded by pinkish white flowers; 'Veitchii' has pinkish purple centers surrounded by white flowers that turn pink with age.

Kerria japonica
JEW'S MANTLE
Height and Spread 6-8 ft/1.8-2.4 m
Most old country gardens seem to include this vigorous and unfussy spring-flowering shrub. It spreads rampantly via suckers, so plant with caution, but its erect, slender, dark green shoots are covered with bright yellow flowers in spring, providing valuable color in slightly shady spots.

Philadelphus spp.
MOCK ORANGE
Height 3-9 ft/1-2.8 m, Spread 3-5 ft/1-1.5 m
If you're restricting yourself to one or two shrubs, include mock orange. This lovely free-flowering bush has an attractive upright habit with soft arching branches and produces gloriously scented, clear white flowers in early to

An arch of Garrya elliptica

midsummer, perfuming a wide area of the garden and also lovely in cut flower arrangements. It grows in any soil in a sunny position. 'Belle Etoile' (height 4 ft/1.2 m, spread 7 ft/2.2 m) has intensely fragrant, single, creamy-white flowers splashed with purple at the center. 'Lemoinei' (height 5 ft/1.5 m) is equally beautifully scented, its flowers pure white with yellow centers; 'Manteau d'Hermine' (height 5 ft/1.5 m) has very fragrant, double, creamy-white blossoms.

Santolina chamaecyparissus
COTTON LAVENDER
Height 12 in./30 cm, Spread 18 in/45 cm
The bright silvery gray leaves of cotton lavender make attractive low hedges for edging herb or flower beds, sometimes used as an alternative to lavender. Like most gray-leaved plants, santolina needs very well-drained, gritty soil and full sunshine. It produces small, yellow, button-headed flowers in summer, but is generally grown for its foliage. It is a good subject for clipping into neat shapes and keeps its form well if you trim bushes in early summer and just tidy them up as necessary in the late fall.

Syringa vulgaris
LILAC
Height 10-13 ft/3-4 m, spread 5-6 ft/1.5-1.8 m
There used to be lilacs in most country gardens; they were deemed to protect the house and keep witches and general bad luck from home and family. Often a gardener planted the sweetly scented, pink-purple-flowered variety on one corner and the white-flowered one on another, but the very fragrant white flowers were never picked for the house because it was believed they would bring death to a member of the family if they came inside. However, the white blossoms were common funeral flowers. Lilacs are slightly untidy bushes if left to their own devices, and they can sucker, so they are probably best in a hedge rather than as specimen large shrubs, although you can keep them under control by cutting them back hard after flowering. In addition to the common lilac, you can find literally hundreds of named varieties with blossoms varying in size and color from deep purplish red to double white, but for popularity, the traditional lilac form is hard to beat.

Teucrium fruticans
GERMANDER
Height and Spread 12-24 in./30-60 cm
This pretty silvery gray-leaved shrub is covered in delicate blue flowers all summer. Like other gray foliage plants, it needs a sunny site and very well-drained soil. It is reliably hardy in cold gardens, but doesn't like prolonged wet.

Viburnum spp.
VIBURNUMS
Height and Spread vary
This huge family includes shrubs for all yards and situations. A favorite for 500 years in traditional European gardens is the popular evergreen *Viburnum tinus* (height and spread 5-6 ft 6 in./1.5-2 m). It forms a generous dense bush with glossy evergreen leaves, and clusters of flat-headed white flowers appear from fall into mid-spring, a time when few plants are giving their best show. Flowers are followed by small, oval, blue-black berries. Some gardeners group several together to form a dense screen; others feel they're best as individual bushes since a large group can look a little stiff and uninteresting once the bright flowers have faded. *Viburnum* x *bodnantense* 'Dawn' is a wonderful upright (height 8-10 ft/2.5-3 m, spread 5 ft/1.5 m) deciduous shrub for winter fragrance, producing intensely scented, dark pink flowers that fade to white. These blossoms are borne prolifically on bare branches from late fall into spring. This shrub responds very well to clipping once it has flowered, and can be trimmed into a canopy shape, perfect for growing bulbs and shade-loving perennials in its shade. *V. farreri* is a highly ornamental upright form (height 3 m/ 10 ft, spread 6 ft 6 in./2 m) with very scented tubular flowers in autumn and winter on bare branches followed by bright red berries. Its long, dark green leaves are bronze when young and turn red-purple in the fall.

Hydrangea macrophylla 'Blue Bonnet'

Philadelphus lemoinei

Syringa vulgaris

Ornamental trees

There is nothing in the garden as uplifting as a tree; don't miss out even if you have very limited space. If you have room for only one tree, plant an apple. If you have space for two trees, make them fruit trees, but then start to consider an ornamental tree or two. Depending on what else is in your yard, you may want a tree that produces beautiful spring blossoms, or vibrant autumn colors; it may be the color or texture of the bark or the shape of the tree that attracts you. Be careful where you site any tree, and take particular account of how tall it will grow and where the shade will fall. Heights listed below represent the approximate final height you can expect your tree to grow. Most will take at least 20 years to reach anywhere near their full height, although the smaller trees (10-15 ft/3-4.5 m) should attain their final height within about 15 years. However, if you really have your heart set on a particular large tree, such as an oak or the splendid tulip tree *(Liriodendron tulipifera)*, there's nothing to stop you from growing one and enjoying it until it outgrows the space, then cutting it down and using the wood. It is your yard, so don't be too swayed by what other people think is appropriate.

Plant trees in large holes, breaking up the base of the hole with a garden fork to encourage water to drain. Settle a few inches of soil gently around the tree's roots; then backfill the hole with the rest of the soil you took out. Firm the tree in well and attach it to a stake about 2 feet (60 cm) tall. Keep newly planted trees well watered. Plant bareroot trees in winter when they are dormant. Container-grown specimens can be planted at any time.

Amelanchier lamarckii
SNOWY MESPILUS, JUNEBERRY
Height 35 ft/11 m

This showy tree maintains interest through the seasons with its changing displays of color, and it is easy to grow in any fertile soil in sun or partial shade, although it dislikes very chalky ground. It produces white flowers in spring among young copper-colored foliage that turns a rich green as leaves mature; red berries appear in early summer, changing to black in June — hence the name. In the fall the green leaves turn to brilliant yellow if the tree is in shade and bright red in a sunny site.

Betula jacquemontii
SILVER BIRCH
Height 50 ft/15 m

Hardy silver birches will eventually grow very tall in the right conditions — a cold climate, moist fertile soil, and a sunny or semi-shady spot — but they are still wonderful in yards, slim, elegant trees with glowing silvery-white bark that pierces the dark dull days of winter. The white bark of *B. papyrifera*, the paper birch or canoe birch — named because it was used for the dugout canoes of Native Americans — peels in thin layers, pale orange brown when first exposed. For maximum effect, plant three silver birches close together in the corner of a yard where they are visible from the house — you can restrict their growth by giving them less-than-ideal conditions and planting close together in this way.

Crataegus spp.
HAWTHORN
Height 25 ft/8 m

If a hawthorn hedge is not for you, consider a member of this family for a specimen tree. Not only do they have attractive blossoms and berries, they also make a neat round-headed shape and are very popular with all sorts of insects and birds. *C. laevigata* 'Paul's Scarlet' bears profuse, double, dark pink flowers on slightly thorny branches; *C. lavallei* 'Carrierei' is a semi-evergreen thorny tree with very glossy dark green leaves; white summer flowers are followed by long-lasting orange-red fruit. *C. mordensis* 'Snowbird' is thornless with very fragrant double white flowers and reddish pink haws. Hawthorns grow best in fertile soil in sunshine, but are very tolerant of most conditions, still putting on a good display.

Cercis siliquastrum
JUDAS TREE
Height 15 ft/5 m

A stunning small tree, producing clusters of bright pink, pealike flowers in spring just as the heart-shaped leaves unfold, beginning bronze, then maturing to blue-green. Flowers are followed by flattened green seed pods that turn red when ripe, and leaves that turn yellow before falling in autumn. Judas trees prefer a sunny spot in well-drained soil and tend to balk at cold clay soils, but are otherwise easy to grow. In a cold yard you may prefer to grow them as climbers, trained against the poles of an arbor or arch. The more you prune them in summer, the more they flower.

Cornus mas
CORNELIAN CHERRY
Height 16 ft/5 m

This is another valuable small tree, with attractive flowers, fruit, and good fall color. The clusters of yellow flowers are produced in late winter before the leaves unfurl. Edible red berries appear in late summer — you have to be quick to get to them before the birds — then leaves turn deep reddish purple in the fall.

Hamamelis spp.

WITCH HAZEL

Height 12 ft/4 m

Witch hazel is a traditional medicinal tree, and ideal for any small yard with its shrubby habit and fragrant, spider-shaped, yellow winter flowers. Witch hazels flourish in a sunny position, but are fully hardy and produce the best displays of flowers in cold, dry winters. *H. mollis* has intensely fragrant, golden yellow flowers on bare branches in mid- and late winter. *H. virginiana* has smaller yellow flowers freely produced from late fall through winter, but these don't have the characteristic scent. Witch hazels have good fall coloring, and they form attractive small trees that make fine shapes in a flowerbed, while providing gentle semi-shade for other plants to grow beneath.

Laburnum watereri 'Vossii'

GOLDEN RAIN, GOLDEN CHAIN TREE

Height 25 ft/8 m

The common laburnum (*L. anagyroides*) used to be one of the trees found most often in European country gardens, grown for its profusion of pendulous clusters of yellow flowers in late spring to early summer, but all parts of the tree are poisonous and it drops masses of seed pods, so a much better choice is *L. watereri* 'Vossii,' which not only forms few seeds but also produces much longer clusters of dense yellow flowers, up to 20 inches (50 cm) long. Laburnum likes a sunny spot.

Malus spp.

CRABAPPLE

Height 16 ft/5 m

The wild crabapple (*Malus sylvestris*) has pretty white flowers followed by reddish yellow fruits, but it's not really worth growing in the yard unless you have a sizeable orchard. Then it's a great addition — its tart fruits make delicious jelly and are a helpful addition to other preserves. But crabapples can be beautiful trees, particularly *M.* 'Golden Hornet' which has pink buds opening to white flowers flushed with pink, and masses of bright yellow ornamental fruits in the fall. Although not productive itself, 'Golden Hornet' is an excellent pollinator for apple trees.

Prunus spp.

FLOWERING CHERRY

Height 16-33 ft/5-10 m

Many of the common flowering cherries available today have originally come from Japan, and would certainly not have been grown in traditional European country gardens, but they make good alternatives to taller native cherries if you're seeking prolific displays of cherry blossom. However, the bird cherry (*Prunus padus*) (height 33 ft/10 m) has been grown for centuries. It is suitable for quite a small yard, and produces blossoms quite different from other cherries. Long pendulous clusters of almond-scented white flowers form in spring, followed by glossy black fruit. *P. subhirtella* 'Autumnalis' (16-20 ft/5-6 m) is covered with clusters of pink-tinged white flowers in periods of mild weather from fall to spring, with a final flush in spring. *P.* 'Mount Fuji' (16 ft/5 m) is one of the most popular Japanese cherries, deservedly so with its arching branches and fragrant snowy white flowers in mid-spring among lovely fresh, dark green foliage.

Sorbus aucuparia

ROWAN OR MOUNTAIN ASH

Height 15-35 ft/5-11 m

No country garden once dared to be without a rowan tree — considered to be a talisman against witchcraft. White spring flowers are followed by clusters of orange berries, delicious in tart jelly, and the delicate, mid-green feathery leaves give the conical-shaped tree a light, open appearance. It is a delicate-looking tree, but very hardy. *S. cashmiriana* has large pink flowers in spring followed by clusters of large white berries; 'Joseph Rock' has bright yellow berries. If you are planting berried trees to attract birds, they will first choose red or orange berries; pink and white ones are low on their list of favorites.

Crataegus laevigata 'Paul's Scarlet'

Laburnum anagyroides

Sorbus 'Joseph Rock'

PERMANENT FEATURES

Reclaimed materials

There's something deeply satisfying about reusing materials to give them a new life. It appeals to a sense of thrift in most of us, and allows us to feel inventive and creative. It is also entirely in the spirit of the country garden, where materials were not bought but found or begged, and make-do–and-mend was the order of the day. As a result, gardens were individual and full of character, even if they were relying on a fairly limited palette of plants and resources. So do hesitate before heading off to the garden center, and see what you can reuse, repair, or recycle.

It is surprising what useful discarded materials you can find if you set out to look. Broken stones or tiles are often left at the end of a construction job, ideal for use in paving and walling. There are plenty of reclamation and salvage yards around, offering everything from garden statuary and troughs to secondhand paving materials, as well as many quirky and beautiful bits and pieces. A rusty old animal feeding or water trough can become an attractive planter, and lengths of old metal guttering can be transformed into planting spaces or path edges.

Reclaimed wood is more problematic. There is no point in making a garden structure from something that will rot very fast, but you can treat sound lumber with preservative, and offcuts of treated softwood are useful in gates and fences or for making a compost bin or tool storage box. Railroad ties make excellent steps or soil retainers in a sloping garden, but use only those that have been weathered in sun and rain for a while since they are often heavily impregnated with oils and creosote, which plants do not appreciate.

Old walling stone is easy to come by in some areas. Even if you don't want walls, stone makes an excellent edging for paths and beds. Old bricks are also easily obtainable, but never use ordinary house bricks for paving — they will crack and flake in the frost.

Left: Any receptacle of sufficient size can be adapted to create a useful container — even an old trash can makes an ideal growing space for potatoes in a small yard.

Right: Discarded roofing tiles or slates make an excellent and decorative wall, while other found pieces of stone and wood add to the rustic feel of this garden.

USING RECLAIMED MATERIALS

■ Scavenged lumber often has a quirky character. If it isn't robust enough for construction, consider pieces as garden sculptures and short-term seating. Don't mix old lumber with new in construction.

■ Never throw away broken roofing slates or tiles as they may be useful for edging or paving.

■ Broken terra cotta pots make good additions to mosaic paving.

■ Keep straight branches and twigs from pruning trees and hedges to use as plant supports or to make rustic arches.

■ Old wooden indoor furniture can be attractive in the garden, painted well to protect it from the weather.

■ Use discarded lengths of chicken wire as supports for climbers and to protect seedlings from birds in the vegetable plot.

■ Remove as much rust as possible from old metal containers, and repaint well to prolong their life as plant pots.

Fences and walls

The materials you use for your boundaries influence the whole feeling of your yard. Your choice will depend on whether you want to maintain a feeling of openness, or whether shelter and privacy are your main priorities. Remember that mixing and matching the materials and heights of your boundaries will soften the edges of a very square or rectangular plot.

Fencing

Simple wooden fences are traditionally found in country gardens and are ideal for a small yard where they define space without blocking open views or erecting solid barriers. They can be cheap as well as versatile. You can buy ready-made panels or make your own to introduce personal variations — for example, vertical pieces can be different heights, and the tops can be cut into simple patterns to give

individual character to your garden. Hardwood such as oak has now become too expensive for most budgets, so if you buy new wood, choose softwood that has been pressure-treated with preservative to ensure it lasts many years. If you re-use scrap wood, treat it thoroughly with an environmentally friendly outdoor wood preservative before making it into fencing — get advice from your garden supplier and never use strong chemical preservatives where you wish to grow plants, especially fruit and vegetables.

The classic American picket fence can be highly ornate with white painted and shaped boards and finials, as seen here, or you can keep it plain with simple stained cut boards, depending on which style suits your situation and garden.

Verbascums, foxgloves, and aquilegias mark a field style boundary.

Passion flowers adorn this painted balustrade-style fence.

BOUNDARIES AT A GLANCE

■ Wooden picket fencing — versatile, cheap, flexible in design and size, and good for plants to scramble through and over. If painted, requires regular maintenance; no privacy.

■ Post and rails — softwood versions are inexpensive and quick to erect, but they offer no privacy and require additional wire to contain or support plants.

■ Ready-made sawn-wood panels — these are inexpensive and can be versatile. Quality is variable, and all must be well mounted; solid barriers can become unstable in windy conditions.

■ Wooden trellis — versatile, excellent support for plants. Fragile, so must be well secured and mounted; no privacy.

■ Local stone — long-lasting and attractive, complementing neighboring buildings and features.

■ Brick — versatile but expensive. Time-consuming to lay.

Train green willow in a lattice pattern for a fast-growing and long-lasting living fence.

Solid wooden fencing is practical and makes an excellent backdrop for climbing plants, but if your garden is particularly windy, always mix solid panels with lengths of sturdy wooden trellis to allow some wind to filter through. Otherwise, you may create a barrier that wind will buffet against and roar over to cause havoc in your garden. Recycled materials such as floorboards make sturdy and richly textured lengths of fencing or screening. Many mass-produced fence panels are poor quality, and will need to be either stained or painted before you erect them, but they fit well into a country garden when they are mixed with other materials.

Where you want instant height at low cost, simply erect fence posts about 8 feet (2.5 m) apart and stretch galvanized wires between them, about 12 inches (30 cm) apart. Attach the wires with staples and use them as a framework for growing climbers or training fruit trees. Soon you will have a living barrier that changes with the seasons. With patience you can weave your own fencing — or screens — from hazel or willow branches. These are very sympathetic in country gardens and provide comfortable support for plants, but they are not particularly long lasting.

Erecting fences

There are two rules: always set fence posts into metal sockets so they won't rot, and then concrete them firmly into the ground. You can use 10 inch (25 cm) lengths of suitably wide old pipes, or buy ready-made sockets. Leave the concrete to harden before attaching horizontals or sections of fencing. The second rule is to erect sections one stretch at a time. Put in one post, measure the panel and dig the second hole and insert the post, attach the section, then concrete in the posts, and continue along the length of your fence. Otherwise, you may well be

unpleasantly surprised to discover that sections seem to shrink between measuring and attaching them to fence posts, and once the posts are firmly in place, it is too late to move them.

Walls

In some areas stone is common, but choose stone walls as boundaries only if they are typical of your area. Otherwise, they will look contrived and out of place. Also, be careful about scale because walls can look dominant and pretentious in some settings, and tall walls can seem fortresslike, unsuitable for a country garden. Always use local stone, because stone from a different area will never blend with the surroundings. Try to follow the regional style of wall building — different areas have unique styles that lend character and a sense of place to a garden. Brick walls are similarly attractive where brick is a typical local building material, and there is a huge variety of brick colors and textures to choose from. Sunny walls make perfect sun traps — low ones will shelter more tender herbaceous plants and taller walls can protect sun-loving fruit trees such as peaches, nectarines, and figs.

Left: This old red brick wall makes a wonderful background to the shades of pinks and reds of perennial geraniums, Knautia macedonica, lavatera, phlox, black hollyhocks, and deep velvety red clematis.

Right: A stone wall will eventually be colonized by mosses and lichens, here contrasting with the bright pink of clambering aubretia.

Gates

If your yard is surrounded by a fence or wall, the choice of gate sets the scene for what visitors can expect to find beyond it, so make the entrance inviting and enticing, while keeping it simple and unpretentious. The proportions are important, and a simple and fairly narrow low gate is still probably the best choice for a country-style garden. If you want to match the height of a tall fence or wall, a low gate

with an arch above it for climbing plants is better than a tall gate or door. These tend to look rather too rigid for a country-garden gateway unless you are entering the yard through a tall informal hedge of different shapes and textures such as hawthorn, damson, and field maple.

A low wooden gate probably remains the most popular and attractive entrance of all to an abundant country garden. Picket gates made of vertical palings are popular, but in a rural area a farm-style wicket gate looks good — different regions traditionally had their own styles and designs, so you may be able to find a gate that gives your yard a real sense of place. Ready-made wooden gates are easy to come by, but it doesn't take much skill to make a gate yourself, with the added advantage that it's usually possible to get materials for nothing and you can add individual touches.

Wrought-iron gates can be very atmospheric, and you can get one made to your specifications without much trouble, but keep the design simple and avoid modern ornate examples, which will always look out of place. You can often pick up rusty old gates that are not hard to reclaim with a bit of elbow grease, plenty of sandpaper and steel wool, followed by careful painting with primer and top coat.

An arch above a low gate adds height and interest, and provides visitors with a sense of anticipation as they walk beneath dripping flowers and foliage. Match the material you use for your arch with your gate, using round poles if your gate is made of round lumber, or sawn wood above picket gates.

Left: Covered with clematis, a thin metal arch is supported on brick pillars surrounding a traditional wooden gate for an entrance that would suit an urban or rural garden.

Right: This simple metal gate allows the plants to speak out, tempting a visitor past the mounds of stachys and valerian, under the abundant roses and into the appealing garden beyond.

GREAT GATES

■ Always use pressure-treated lumber or treat wood for outside use with a preservative, and drill holes before hammering in nails to avoid splitting the wood.

■ If your fence is made from flat sawn pieces of wood, use flat planks for the gate.

■ A gate in a rustic woven fence or a hedge can be made from short sections of round wood, even stakes, or split fence posts.

■ A low gate suits a high fence or hedge.

■ Arches over gateways can be as simple as two metal hoops or a pair of bound branches.

Arches and arbors

Arches are a fairly staple element of a country garden, used most often to add height and interest above gates and over straight paths, while providing an attractive frame for the yard beyond. They are usually clothed with climbing plants, although a simple unclothed rustic arch can also make an attractive feature among a sea of lower plants.

Traditional arches over gates range from ornate wooden structures that resemble European church lychgates to simple metal hoops. Arches made from found wood or woven branches are popular, attractive, and functional. Your choice probably depends largely on whether you want to make it yourself or buy ready-made. Growing arches formed by

training trees are very suitable for a country garden; a yew arch at an entrance or a fruiting arch over a path are both very inviting,

If you use an arch as a climbing frame, choose the plants according to the type of arch you've erected. The simplest arch of poles covered with chicken wire makes a very effective support and will look stunning in summer when covered with flowers and foliage, but it might appear rather uninspiring in winter months, so climbers such as evergreen honeysuckle and winter clematis are a good choice, where suitable for your climate.

Constructing an arch

When making any wooden structure, particularly something out of found lumber that may have a fairly short life, decide on its position, then concrete four (or more) supporting 2x2 inch (5x5 cm) posts 24 inches (60 cm) long into metal sleeves into the ground, leaving about 8 inches (20 cm) showing; concrete them firmly and attach the arch structure to them. When the main posts of your arch rot, they can then be replaced with minimal disturbance to the plants that will be covering them.

The width and depth of your arch will depend on its position, but try to make it at least 18 inches (45 cm) deep, and preferably more, to allow for a profusion of climbing plants. Unless you are using extremely sturdy posts such as gateposts for the uprights, you should allow for two vertical wooden uprights at least 3 inches (7.5 cm) in diameter on each side of an arch, or the finished structure will be too flimsy to support strong climbers.

Left: The soft apricot Rosa 'Buff Beauty' is joining old-fashioned scented pink and white roses to clothe the plain metal arch that will frame the view into the field beyond the garden.

Right: The hard lines of a wide arch of latticed lumber should be softened by covering it with foliage and blossoms, such as the deliciously scented Rosa 'Madame Caroline Testout'.

Arbors

When you've been working hard to create a beautiful garden, there's little that is more pleasurable than sitting in the middle of your plants and admiring it all, or just dreaming — a plant-covered sitting space is a lovely addition to any garden. An arbor covered with scented flowers can be an incurably romantic spot, and it is also good use of space in a small yard, providing seating, shade, and a spot for climbers.

The simplest are easily constructed rustic wooden arches with seats beneath, or you can make fancy structures from planks. Always use pressure-treated sawn wood or treated rustic poles so your arbor lasts as long as possible. The height and width are important — if you surround an arbor with scented roses, make sure there is enough room to sit without fearing scratches.

Planting rules

Dig the ground well at the base of the supports to two spade's depth, and add plenty of manure and compost before planting. Try to give plants as much space as possible at the base of each pole so they grow freely — a straggly, unhappy specimen feebly trying to climb an arch is a pathetic sight. The most traditional plants are roses, honeysuckle, and clematis, and of course sweet peas, but you don't have to stick to convention — climbing gourds and squash are fun, particularly when grown with nasturtiums, and morning glories and green beans make excellent climbing companions.

When choosing roses remember that ramblers climb more vigorously than climbers, but only blossom convincingly once, while many climbing roses flower repeatedly. Be aware that the most rampant roses will require a great deal of tying in and cutting back, and may become irritating in a confined space but are perfect where they can continue from an arch along a hedge or fence. There are similarly wide varieties of clematis to choose from, but the most vigorous *C. montana* varieties produce so much growth that they can become a nuisance. Honeysuckle is an obvious choice and mixes well with roses or clematis.

In a larger garden you can create an informal long walk by erecting a series of wooden arches along a slightly winding gravel path, softened further by generous plantings on either side.

FRUITING ARCHES

Winter is the time to construct a tree-training arch as you must plant bare-rooted trees. You can use quite flimsy poles to make an arch from four posts at least 3 feet (1 m) apart, and plant four fruit trees at their bases, into well-manured soil. Choose semi-dwarfing rootstocks, and if you are having mixed fruit, make sure each tree is self-pollinating. Tie the trees to the arch framework and prune them as single stem cordons (see page 43). When the tops of the trees meet, you can cut off the growing tips and tie them together.

1

2a

2b

TRAINING A FRUITING ARCH

1 Construct a simple arch with four supports 3 feet (1 m) apart (see page 143). Plant four trees on semi-dwarfing rootstocks and train them as cordons (see page 43). If you are having mixed fruit, be sure to choose self-pollinating varieties.

3

2 Years Two and Three
In the first winter, cut back any side shoots to four buds (**2a**). In the second and third winters, cut sub-laterals (new side shoots) back to 1 inch (2.5 cm) from their starting point (**2b**). Don't allow fruit to ripen in the second and third years, so remove flowers in spring.

3 Year Four on
Once you have the desired shape, tie the tops of each tree together and prune them to shape in summer to encourage fruiting and reduce vigor. You may need to prune them slightly in winter, removing unwanted shoots.

Paths and steps

The appearance of a path can affect the look of everything around it, while its design and placement is crucial to satisfactory use of your yard. So choose materials for your paths with consideration and construct them with care — they are permanent structures.

Paths between the main areas of your yard, and from the entrance to the house, will take a lot of wear and tear from feet, wheel barrows, and perhaps bicycles. They need to be very solidly made from durable materials, although you may be able to get away with grass or beaten earth paths to less well-used areas. Any path leading to the front or back door needs to be solid near the house, so you don't traipse mud indoors. In areas that get little traffic, set stepping stones into grass — these can be random stones, square slabs, or even log slices.

Construction

A well-constructed path consists of three distinct layers: a membrane to allow water to drain away and prevent mud from forming, followed by a layer of gravel or sand to supply strength to resist the pressure of traffic and to provide support for the top layer of surface material such as paving stones. Dig the trench for your path a minimum 6 inches (15 cm) deep for gravel or paving stones, 8 inches (20 cm) for bricks, and about 12 inches (30 cm) for cobblestones — put valuable topsoil aside to reuse elsewhere, in raised beds, for example, or to improve areas of poor soil.

Lay woven polypropylene sheet — landscape fabric — directly onto the soil as the membrane, allowing a 2 inch (5 cm) overlap to curl up each side of the trench. On top of this, spread a minimum 4 inch (10 cm) layer of scalpings, gray fragments of dust, and crushed building stone — available very cheaply from gravel quarries. If your top surface is brick, slate, or stone, lay at least 2 inches (5 cm) of scalpings and 2 inches (5 cm) of sand to bed the materials on. For cobbles, you need 4 inches (10 cm) of scalpings followed by 4 inches (10 cm) of sand, because the cobbles must be buried to half their height in sand, tapped carefully and firmly into place with a rubber mallet, then have sand brushed into the gaps before being finished off with a sand and cement mixture.

Always firm a cobblestone, brick, or stone surface by working across it with a heavy piece of wood, hammering the wood as you go, rather than hitting the materials directly, then brush a dry mix of sand and cement into the cracks, which should then be watered and left to set for 24 hours before you walk on your path.

Left: Gravel paths should be contained with boards sunk to the height of the finished path to prevent gravel spilling onto adjacent beds.

Right: The slightly irregular shapes of old bricks lend themselves to generous spacing, but be sure to fill the gaps completely with a dry sand and cement mix, dampened well with a watering can.

PATHS MADE EASY

■ Try to keep your materials and patterns simple and in keeping with the spirit of the country garden.

■ Don't worry if you can't afford to do everything at once. Start with a simple gravel path and change it later if you need to.

■ Preparation saves problems later on. Always lay paths on a firmed soil base with a layer of sand or sand and cement directly below the path.

■ It is easy to edge a path with boards to keep earth off the path and gravel off your soil or grass.

■ Bricks make attractive and very traditional paths, but make sure you choose hard stock; house bricks tend to flake in frost.

■ Cobbles or pebbles match the informality of a country garden and make beautiful patterns and textures. Never take pebbles from a beach without permission.

Two traditional, country-style patterns often used when laying brick paths or patio areas.

Materials

Gravel is an obvious choice where your budget is limited, or for a temporary surface until you can create something more permanent. Available in many different colors and grades, it is perfectly in keeping with a country-garden style, can be laid with minimal preparation, and lasts well if it is contained by edging. Spread 2 inches (5 cm) above 4 inches (10 cm) of scalpings and tamp it down well to avoid carrying it into the house on your shoes. You have to keep it weeded by hand, but many welcome plants will happily self-seed into gravel.

Natural flagstones or stone slabs look wonderful in any path, and combine beautifully with plants. If a plain stone path feels a bit formal, mix slabs with slate, cobblestones or recycled tiles or bricks for an attractive, textured, and lasting path, or surround them with gravel. When laying mixed materials, be careful to keep the levels even. It's easy to find reconstituted stone slabs, but they really don't look the same as the real stuff and can be hard to blend into a country garden. Cobblestones are traditional, economical, and hard-wearing, and make a perfect foil for plants; they're best for small areas or sections of path since they take some time to lay. You can make detailed patterns and mosaics with cobblestones mixed with pebbles or pieces of slate and stone. Slate provides striking contrasts to softer textured and colored materials, but it gets slippery after rain and frost, so use it with care.

Bricks are still a popular choice. They are easy to lay on a bed of sand above scalpings, small enough to be easy to arrange for curves and corners, and they lend themselves to patterns and shapes in restricted spaces. But always be sure to use frost-resistant bricks or special pavers, as ordinary house bricks will flake and crack.

Edging paths

It is a good idea to edge a path to keep materials from shifting, and to restrain soil from adjacent beds. A cheap and easy solution is to use lengths of pressure-treated lumber, 3 inches (7.5 cm) wide and 1 inch (2.5 cm) thick, anchored with pegs before the top surface is laid. Knock 12 inch (30 cm) pegs, made of the same wood, into the ground, leaving 2 inches (5 cm) showing, and nail the edging boards to these.

However, you may be able to use up leftover materials for your edges. Half bricks are traditional, particularly common to edge cobblestone paths, but quirkier materials work just as well. For example, rows of upended glass bottles, sunk into the ground, are durable, functional, and interesting.

You can buy copies of specially made Victorian rope-edged tiles, which look best if you restrict their use rather than edging every path or bed with them. Miniature "hurdles" have made an appearance in recent years, but they are more decorative than functional because they really don't last long in contact with soil and foliage. Step-over fruit trees make an unusual and productive edging to paths that pass through a kitchen garden.

Steps

Some yards have steep banks where steps are a necessity; others seem almost entirely flat but will probably include slight rises and falls where you might wish to insert a step or two to introduce changes in level that add to any garden's interest. The placement and design of steps is crucial. Even in steep gardens you need step-free areas for wheeling barrows and carts, and it is always best to make shallow, broad steps that look generous and expansive, and feel comfortable and secure.

In a gravel path, gravel treads contained by wooden risers are cheap, functional, and fit the style; stone and brick steps fit most situations, but need careful construction with solid foundations. Old railroad ties are secure and easy to install but look best in grass or semi-wild areas, so they don't fit into all country gardens.

STEPS CHECKLIST

■ Broad treads and shallow risers
are more comfortable, safe, and
attractive than steep, narrow steps.

■ Broad steps make an area feel
less cramped, open up the space,
and can also be used by more than
one person at a time.

■ Curved steps add interest to a
square or oblong garden.

■ On a steep bank, steps that
cross the slope rather than going
straight down are more pleasant
to use.

■ When using bricks or stone, be
careful not to choose materials that
flake after frost or become slippery
when wet.

■ Contained gravel steps are
suitable for shady areas where
other materials become slippery.

*Steps don't have to be straight. Here
shallow circular steps from bricks and
pebbles make a decorative transition —
complete with small fountain — from
one level to another.*

Dining areas and outdoor furniture

Your yard is there to be enjoyed — all its scents, shapes, colors, wildlife, and the many little touches that make it so personal. For many people somewhere to sit outside and read or entertain is just as important as frothing flowerbeds and flourishing produce. A seating area might be as simple as a couple of kitchen chairs and a temporary table in a sunny spot outside the back door, or you may opt for a specific area with more permanent seating and eating arrangements.

The site is obviously the most important thing. Make sure your seat catches the sun at the time of day you'll be able to enjoy it, and allows the possibilities of shade, privacy, and shelter. You may find several favorite spots for different times of day and seasons. Some may be

Left: A dining area can be as simple as a painted table and chairs placed directly onto the grass in a sunny corner, Here it is delineated by a painted post and rails leading to a shed completely hidden in a profusion of scented roses.

Below: Place a bench where you can best appreciate your favorite part of the garden and sit surrounded by your flowers.

special quiet places, or spots where you and your family can catch the morning sun before going about your daily business; others will be for entertainment. If you're starting from scratch, be patient. Don't rush to erect a solid wall for shelter and privacy; woven willow or hazel panels, planted arbors, or growing screens are more in keeping with a country garden, and a well-placed tree will eventually provide substantial solid or dappled shade.

A small, intimate space surrounded by growing plants works very well within a small country garden, but whatever the size of your sitting area, it is wise to lay some kind of solid surface if you plan to use it much. Try to use the same style of materials as your path to keep a sense of unity; and never make paved areas too hard or harsh, or they risk looking like suburban patios rather than integral parts of an informal garden. Simplicity is the key, and some of the most effective country garden sitting-out areas are surfaced simply with a few bricks or patches of cobblestones set into gravel. Plant herbs such as thyme and marjoram between bricks or paving stones, or into gravel; every time you brush against them, their aroma will scent the area.

If you decide on a permanent barbeque structure, don't make it too dominant, and construct it from sympathetic materials. It is a good idea to be able to cover it to turn it into a useful table that can be used for potting or other garden tasks, or for supporting decorative containers. Single slabs of slate or stone make attractive but hefty covers, or perhaps a piece of marble from an old greenhouse. Otherwise, a sheet of metal is functional, or cover a piece of wood with roofing felt to create an all-weather surface.

Outdoor furniture

Wooden furniture is deservedly popular, but when you buy new pieces, they often arrive a disagreeable orange color, so it is a good move to stain or paint them so they can sit more happily in their surroundings. Conventional country-garden seats are very simply made from round-cut rustic poles. You can buy or find the poles, but make sure they are treated with preservative before pieces are nailed together, and always drill the wood first to prevent it from splitting.

Outdoor seats and tables can be totally individual and provide great opportunities for inventive scavenging and recycling. Old chairs can get a new life for several years outdoors with a few licks of paint, as long as you put them away in winter; logs or old railroad ties become attractive seats in a shady spot, a wooden barrel can be turned into a comfortable seat by cutting away the front and inserting a plank to sit on; with a little imagination, bits of boats and old tin bathtubs can be converted into handsome seats, as well as carpenter's fantasies and living chairs made from woven hazel and willow. A table can be as simple as a board placed on top of a few upturned flowerpots, a piece of stone atop a column, or piles of round-cut logs used as supports. Be as quirky or inventive as you like: even without carpentry skills it can cost you very little to provide attractive and functional seats and tables. Never be tempted to go for the cheapest garden-center offerings to save money. Mass-produced plastic and cheap metal furniture will spoil even the most beautifully planted country garden.

Far left: This unusual seat is made from found rustic lumber surrounded by woven hazel, which also acts as an informal support for sweet peas and a boundary to restrain the overflowing plants behind.

Left: A charming garden seat constructed from recycled materials by an inventive carpenter.

Right: Nothing could be simpler than a chair placed in the middle of the profusion of flowers and scents that make up this wonderfully informal country garden.

Ponds

While it is doubtful that a garden pool would have been a priority for early country gardeners, a pond makes one of the most satisfying additions to any yard. Certainly if you are choosing between an area of grass or water, go for water every time: it can divide the space in much the same way as an area of grass but additionally, brings light and movement and attracts all sorts of animals, insects, and birds into your yard. Apart from the ecological benefits, the sight and sound of water brings another dimension to the way you experience your garden — another place to dream and let your imagination wander.

Since a country garden is all about abundance and diversity, think about your pond in terms of the variety of creatures it can attract, as well as the planting opportunities it offers. While bigger is definitely better in these terms, even a tub of water can make a difference, attracting birds and insects and perhaps frogs. If you want pumped moving water, choose the fountain or feature carefully. Remember that in country gardens, simplest really is the best.

You don't need a natural source of water to have a pond, but you are blessed if your property boasts an existing stream or spring. When you are introducing water from scratch, there are two fundamental considerations when choosing where to place your pond: you need as level a site as possible or you will need to level it, and a pond needs sunlight and shade so site the pond in a sunny spot that is shadowed for part of the day. The shadow falling from a wall or fence, or from large-leaved plants around the edges is ideal; if there is a partial canopy from a deciduous tree, you must clear leaves from the pond when they drop in the fall because as they rot they release a gas that can harm some pond life. And of course it's best if you can place a pond where it can be seen or heard from the house or from convenient outdoor areas.

Traditional country garden plants including delphiniums and foxgloves, meadowsweet and lychnis, geraniums, iris, and hostas sit happily alongside the dramatic leaves of gunnera, all creeping over the edges of this informal pond.

The best ponds have deep and shallow areas, clear water, and places hidden and shaded by leaves or rocks. The depth of the pond dictates what will live and grow there; 30-40 inches (80-100 cm) is a good depth for water lilies *(Nymphaea spp.)* and many water plants, and deep enough to prevent the very marked temperature changes that can occur in shallow pools. Shallow shelves at the edge of a pond 8-18 inches (20-45 cm) deep provide good environments for a wide range of moisture-loving plants. Gently sloping sides and boggy pond sides are inviting for many whispering grasses, delicate ferns, and ornamentals that provide cover for creatures entering and leaving the water, and visual links between pond and surroundings.

Constructing a pond

There's a wide range of materials to choose from when you install a pond. Check with your local garden center to find out what is the best type to install to withstand the weather in your area. The simplest to install are those made from preformed fiberglass, which is tough and durable. These liners are, however, relatively expensive and come in a fairly limited choice of shapes, and because they don't provide a naturally friendly surface for plants and other pond life, they can take a while to blend in and need careful planting around them. They're probably best avoided in very cold gardens because they may crack if the water freezes solid in winter.

If you're making a pond in solid ground with no risk of settlement, you can build a concrete shell in any shape you wish, which should last for decades if it is well constructed. You must coat the concrete well with waterproof sealant before you fill the pond with water. In some areas you can line a pond with clay, which must be well "puddled," which means firming the base and edges by treading the clay until it is completely smooth. Clay is the best base for plant and pond life, but it is viable only where it's a local material; and clay-lined ponds must never be allowed to dry out, or the clay will crack and water drain away. Once cracks have appeared, clay-lined ponds are difficult to repair.

Probably the easiest choice for most people is a flexible liner of polypropylene. Dig your pond to the size and shape you want, then cover the sides and base with a 2 inch (5 cm) layer of sand or carpet underfelt to prevent small sharp stones from puncturing the liner. Lay the liner over the prepared hole and pull it taut as you fill the pond with water. Don't trim the edges until the pond is completely full, and leave an overlap of 12 inches (30 cm) all around the top. For a soft edge, disguise the liner's edges by surrounding the pond with grass, or by planting to the edge with leafy plants, which will be reflected in the water. In paving, lay flat stones, tiles, or slates on top of the liner on a bed of wet mortar, so they overhang the edge of the pond by 2 inches (5 cm). Maintenance is rarely a problem as long as you don't let the pond dry out and expose the liner to prolonged sunshine.

Carex, Arum lilies, iris, kingcups, and primula colonize the boggy area beside this small pond.

PERENNIALS FOR DAMP POND EDGES

Where a man-made pond has steep sides and doesn't provide a natural damp area, create a link between the water and soil by channeling some water to keep the surroundings damp at all times.

Caltha palustris
Marsh marigolds or kingcups flower very early in spring, providing a bright splash of color at the edge of ponds; they're best in fairly wild gardens. The compact

white form *C. palustris* var. *alba* is ideal beside small ponds.

Filipendula ulmaria
Meadowsweet was once grown as part of every country-garden pharmacy to ease fevers and pains. This hardy plant is also suitable for semi-shady damp beds. Small, perfumed, creamy-white flowers cover the plant from midsummer until fall, and it spreads from creeping rhizomes.

Hemerocallis spp.
Day lilies are perfectly happy growing submerged in 2-4 inches (5-10 cm) of water, in sun or semi-shade.

Hosta spp.
Hostas make an excellent groundcover for pond margins, providing hiding places for all sorts of small creatures. They are unlikely to be troubled by slugs once frogs have colonized your pond.

Iris spp.
Among the hundreds of iris suitable for damp plantings, three old species stand out. *Iris pseudacorus* (3-4 ft/90-120 cm), the broad-leaved yellow flag iris, grows in clumps beside ponds and rivers, and is ideal for any pond edge. *I. pseudacorus* 'Flore Pleno' has a double flower. *Iris versicolor* (24-36 in./60-90 cm), the blue flag, has violet-blue flowers and very bright green leaves. *Iris sibirica*, Siberian iris (30-36 in./75-90 cm), forms erect tufts of narrow leaves and violet-blue flowers in cool wet situations.

Ligularia spp.
The broad, copper-veined, toothed green leaves of ligularia form a decorative clump more than 3 feet (1 m) wide, from which emerge magnificent yellow spikes up to 5 feet (1.5 m) tall in late summer. You can grow them in beds in rich, damp soil, but they come into their own near water.

Pennisetum villosum
In a reasonably sheltered situation, try to include a clump of feathertop grass (6-8 ft/1.8-2.5 m) with its fine blue-green foliage crowned in the fall with bottlebrush white flower spikes.

Primula spp.
Primulas love rich, damp soil, and don't mind wet feet. Candelabra types suit ponds. *P. denticulata* (12 in./30 cm) has spherical blue-purple to red flowers on tall stems in early summer. *P. beesiana* (20-24 in./50-60 cm) produces deep mauve flowers in early summer and self-seeds prolifically. *P. japonica*, Japanese primula (3 ft/1 m), bears tall stems with circles of flowers in shades of pink and blue from late spring to midsummer.

Myosotis palustris
Water forget-me-nots (8-16 in./20-40 cm) are happy around any garden pond.

Veronica beccabunga
Creeping brooklime looks like small blue-flowered watercress. Although its flowers seem insignificant, the deep green leaves remain evergreen when submerged.

Greenhouses

Traditional country gardeners had to make do with germinating plants on a sunny windowsill or planting straight into the ground when the weather allowed, but as soon as mass-produced glass became readily available — from the late 19th century — rudimentary greenhouses sprang up in even the humblest of gardens. A greenhouse really can transform the experience of gardening in a cool climate, allowing you to work in the garden in rotten spring weather, to get a headstart with vegetables and annual flowers each year, and to grow a few tender species in even the coldest areas.

You'll want to nip in and out, so try to place a greenhouse reasonably close to the house, and near a faucet or water barrel. Choose a level site in the open to make sure plants get maximum light at all times. It doesn't really matter whether you position it east-west or north-south, but put the door on the most sheltered side. It's usually best to make a solid floor from a slab of concrete or paving, but you can simply leave soil with a path down the middle. It depends what you want to grow. If vegetables are your passion, you'll need some benches for space for trays of germinating seeds and pots of seedlings. Because you can't grow the same species each year in the same soil, you're better off with pots, growing bags, or built beds to grow them to maturity. Tomatoes, cucumbers, peppers, eggplant, and melons are greenhouse favorites. But if you use yours largely for ornamentals or tender fruit such as grapes or tender varieties of fig, permanent soil will be fine as long as you keep it well-fed with compost and aged manure.

Greenhouses have a reputation for attracting pests, but as long as you keep your plants healthy, your pots clean, and your greenhouse well ventilated so that air can flow through, you'll be fine. Be vigilant and keep an eye out for pests so you can obliterate them before they build up. Aphids are the most common offenders; as soon as you see signs, wipe or spray them off the plants with water, or vacuum them off.

In cooler climates a greenhouse allows you to grow tomatoes, peppers, and eggplants successfully as well as start tender annuals and vegetables early in the season and nurture fall-sown perennials over the winter.

INDOOR TOMATOES

1 Loosely tie the tomato plant with soft garden twine to a cane for support.

2 As the plant grows, remove the side shoots that develop in the angles between the leaves and stems of each leaf while they are still small, or they will use up valuable nutrients.

3 When the plant begins to set fruit, cut off the lower leaves. Remove yellowing or decaying leaves on sight, and when six or seven trusses of fruit have formed, remove the top growing point.

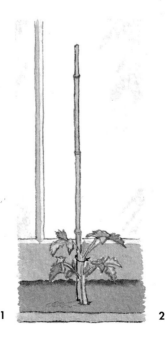

1   2   3

Tools and utilities

Today garden centers and hardware stores offer dozens of kinds of tools that you may be encouraged to think you can't live without, but you can. When you're starting out, purchase a few of the basics that have been used for centuries. They'll become good friends, and if you look after them well, you may find they last you a gardening lifetime. Most important are a good spade and fork and a hand fork and trowel; you'll need a sturdy wheelbarrow, a watering can, a rake, a stiff brush, and a sturdy pair of pruners. The rule is always to buy the best you can afford; stainless steel is hard wearing, easy to keep clean, and somehow more satisfying to use than cheaper spades and forks. Make sure your spade and fork are the right length for you — particularly important if you're rather tall. Nothing will give you a backache quicker than digging with too short a spade. Handles on hand tools must be comfortable to use and well secured. If you're growing vegetables, you'll find a hoe is useful to weed between the rows, but you won't need one in a very damp climate where you must hand weed to pull out miscreants rather than simply chopping off their heads.

Below left: A good fork is the most important tool of all. Choose one with a stainless steel head and a handle the right length for comfort.

Below right: The other garden essential is a sturdy wheelbarrow the right size for your garden so that you can comfortably navigate paths and beds.

Right: A functional tool shed can be as informal and decorative as the rest of your country garden; this reclaimed shed looks at home nestling into the hedge beside the kitchen garden.

Always clean your tools when you finish work, and put them away. It's easy to fill a wooden box with sand to which you've added a bit of oil; every time you come in from working, plunge the blade of your tool into the sandbox. The handles on good tools wear out faster than the tools themselves. Prolong their life by rubbing wooden handles with linseed oil two or three times a year.

If your soil is particularly stony, you'll need to sharpen your spade from time to time, and pruners must be kept oiled and sharp. Not only is trying to use blunt tools irritating, but you create vulnerable spots for disease to enter if you wound plants as you prune them.

You'll need somewhere dry for storage. A toolshed can be an attractive addition to any property, but less beautiful structures can easily be camouflaged while providing additional vertical space for growing climbers. Ideally, organize your shed so tools hang on specific nails, both for convenience and so you can see at a glance if something

is missing and retrieve it. In the smallest spaces there may not be room for a shed, in which case use a wooden box, its top covered with roofing felt for protection, or create storage space under a bench.

Water and compost

Plants need water and rainwater suits them best, so include a rain barrel to catch what you can. Situate it so a downpipe from a gutter on your house or a shed will fill it up. You can improvise with a plastic trash can, but a barrel with its own tap is a good investment. Make sure it is raised off the ground enough to be able to put a watering can comfortably underneath it. Always keep your rain barrel covered to keep the water fresh longer, and so insects can't lay their eggs there.

Another must-have is a compost area. There are different ways to produce compost, but the most practical for most people is cool composting, which means allowing waste materials to rot down in a container for several months. Old-fashioned gardens often included a simple compost heap, but a custom-made box or bin is more space-efficient, and arguably makes better compost, too. Although your compost is an important part of the garden, you probably won't want it in full view of the house or sitting-out areas, but make sure it is easy to get to from the house or you won't put your scraps onto it. Wheelbarrow access must also be good. A plastic compost bin does a good job and can be hidden anywhere, but if you want to make a more traditional compost bin, avoid siting it anywhere in a permanent draft or deep shade, or it will struggle to maintain its moisture and temperature, and too sunny a site will dry it out too quickly.

Compost can be made in any container that allows air to flow in and out and can keep moisture and heat in and cold and rain out. You can use old trash cans, discarded wooden pallets, dumped building materials, or you can buy a plastic bin. Traditional compost bins — open-topped square boxes with slatted fronts so you can get at your compost easily — are still popular. Site your bin straight onto the ground rather than onto a hard surface so earthworms and other soil organisms can get to work as soon as possible.

Every gardener should conserve water by placing a rain barrel below a gutter to catch rainwater, which plants prefer to tap water.

COMPOST BINS

Every country garden – whatever its size – should have a compost bin. The traditional wooden double bin shown below provides the best set-up, but if space is a problem, choose from one of the three smaller alternatives illustrated here.

1 TRADITIONAL DOUBLE BIN

Drive six 5-foot (1.5-m) posts into the ground in three lines 3 feet 6 inches (1.25 m) apart.Nail wooden boards to the stakes to make an E-shaped, open-fronted box with 2-inch (5-cm) gaps between the boards. Use scrap wood if you can — old pallets are ideal.Hammer two 5-foot (1.5-m) stakes 4 inches (10 cm) away from the two open ends of the box.Cut boards to fit and slot them behind the front stakes.Fill one box first so compost can be maturing in the first box while you fill the second.

2 SECTIONAL BIN

Cut twenty 8-inch (18-cm) long blocks of 2-inch (5-cm) square wood. Make five separate squares by nailing 6x36-inch (15x100-cm) boards to the blocks, leaving a stump on each side. Place the first square on the ground and fill it with composting materials, then add the next. There will be a 2-inch (5-cm) gap between the sections to allow air to circulate. When the box is full, cover it with a square of carpet until the compost is ready to use.

2

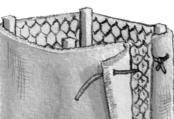

3

3 WIRE BINS

Drive four 4-ft (1.2-m) posts into the ground to make a 36-inch (1-m) diameter circle or square, and wrap chicken wire around them. Insulate with cardboard inside or wrap old carpet round the outside, and cover the top with carpet.

4 RECYCLED BINS

Old oil drums are perfect for compost, but make sure they have been thoroughly cleaned to remove all oil residues. Drill a few holes in the sides to encourage aeration. Old trash cans are perfect for compost too. Drill a few holes in the sides of metal or plastic cans, and take the bottoms out.

1

4

Building for birds

From the earliest days of country gardens, when a pig and chickens were an integral part of the household economy, people, plants, and wildlife have always existed side-by-side in country gardens. Today, few of us keep more than household pets, but the spirit of country gardening means encouraging other creatures into the yard to add to the general abundance and diversity — happy the gardener who works away with a robin or cardinal for company. A garden crammed with a wide range of plants will attract birds, insects, and small mammals and should provide some winter shelter, but there are times when birds in particular need a little help, and bird tables, baths, and boxes are attractive as well as practical additions to any country garden.

If you make your own bird table, steer clear of wood that has been chemically treated, and don't use silver birch because woodpeckers search for food behind the bark of old birch trees and are likely to peck a birch table to pieces in record time! Whatever the design, position your bird table with care. You want to be able to see it from a window to enjoy your visitors, and near enough the house to make sure you keep filling it in even the worst weather when birds need extra food most. Different bird species have different feeding habits, and you should provide a variety of foods. Bird feeders full of nuts do attract dozens of species, but some favor fat first; some love pieces of cheese; others like hard seeds as well as nuts or apples, and soft fruit on the ground rather than the table. If cats are a menace, put an inverted metal cone around the leg of your table; make it high enough to prevent even the most agile feline from leaping up it, or hang the feeder to swing from a branch if there's a convenient tree. Squirrels can be a fearful nuisance; the best way to stop them from stealing all the food is to buy special squirrel-proof bird feeders to hang from tables or branches.

Birds must have water for drinking and bathing, and a birdbath is another country garden essential if you don't have a shallow pond. It only needs to hold an inch or two of water, but it must have very gently sloping sides so the smallest birds can bathe without risk of drowning. Old stone troughs are particularly lovely, but even a plastic trash can lid sunk into the ground surrounded with low-growing plants will do the job. But do make sure any plant cover is not so dense that marauding cats can hide in it and lie in wait.

Far left: Sunflower seeds are a favorite food for finches while the coconut is preferred by tits.
Middle left: An old baking tray stuck on an upright pole makes an instant bird table.
Left: Peanuts should always be provided in a mesh feeder rather than spread on a flat surface.

BIRD BOXES

If you don't have hedges or dense shrubs in your yard, you can still attract resident birds by putting up nesting boxes — perfect on climber-covered walls away from full sun. Different birds need different types of nest sites. The simplest boxes are flat, open trays, 4-6 inches (10-15 cm) square with a 1-inch (2.5-cm) rim around the edge, mounted 3-4 feet (90-120 cm) high on a wall surrounded by climbers; these will attract many birds if there's plenty of cover.

The most common nesting box looks like a closed box with a small hole in it. The size of the hole determines who moves in. A tiny hole just 1.25 inches (3 cm) in diameter will allow house wrens to live there in peace; go up to 1.75 inches (3.3 cm) and chickadees can take over; a 2-inch (5-cm) hole means sparrows could use the box, and so on. Birds often adjust the size of the entrance to suit them, so bird boxes should be made from unstained, rough-cut wood.

Any small wooden box with a hole serves as a nesting box, but handy carpenters can make elaborate boxes and birdtables. Birch should be avoided because woodpeckers will destroy it to get at the grubs that live inside it.

Topiary

Gardeners have never been able to resist dressing up the basics, and topiary provides a wonderful opportunity to show off talent, individuality, and ingenuity. Originally practiced in grand gardens, it was adopted early by cottage gardeners who made it their own — training and trimming their hedges into intricate shapes, clipping arches over gates and doorways, and making freestanding trees into living sculptures. Shrubs such as rosemary and lavender were also often clipped into shapes, but while hedges and trees were sheared by men, shaping herbs into balls and mounds could only be achieved by women — otherwise, it was believed bad luck would haunt the house.

Virtually any small-leaved evergreen tree can be used for topiary, but the most popular are box *(Buxus sempervirens)* and yew *(Taxus baccata)*. Holly is also excellent. Geometric shapes have always been popular — cubes, pyramids, spheres, and cones — as well as animals and birds. Peacocks were the most popular cottage-garden figures.

Training and trimming

It is best to start from scratch by planting a two-year-old tree or shrub in spring into very well-fed and mulched moisture-retentive soil. To form a well-furnished base, trim the bush in late summer, leaving growing points untouched, but trimming back all side shoots hard to encourage a thick hedgelike base. In subsequent years, trim more lightly, aiming to produce the required shape. You need to create a neat solid base before attempting to create a fancy figure such as a peacock. For a square or conical shape, you can leave a number of leaders; for a spiral or cake stand shape, you need to select just one.

Once the framework of any figure is established, you need to prune it once a year in late summer, although some shrubs need cleaning up a little at other times, and lavender and rosemary are best cut back after flowering. For simple geometric shapes you can use powered hedge trimmers; otherwise, use very sharp shears. And you must cut bay with pruners to avoid leaving ugly jagged leaves.

A ball-topped yew spiral under construction adds height and interest in a perennial border.

PEACOCK TOPIARY

The peacock is a traditional topiary shape for country gardens.

1 Insert a stake or stout bamboo pole into the center of the yew bush, and attach a hooped wire framework to it. Use a length of heavy gauge wire for the main shape, and stretch thinner wire in the tail shape for added support. Tie new growth to the framework with thin garden wire.

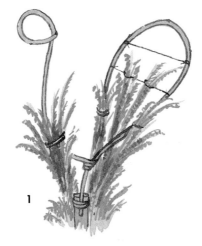

1

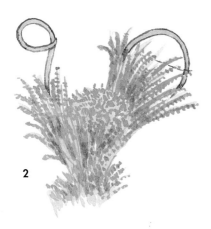

2

2 As the yew grows, keep tying new growth into the framework, then trim the shape around the frame as necessary. Depending on the size of your peacock, it can take several years for the shape to form satisfactorily, and you must be vigilant about tying in new growth several times a year.

3 When the finished shape is reached, you may be able to cut out the wire frame and take out the stake; the bird will not be damaged if they are not removed.

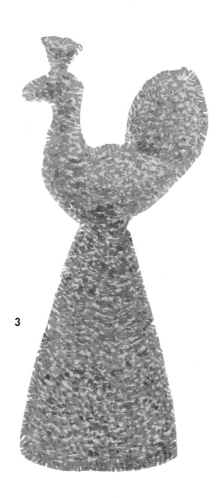

3

USEFUL ADDRESSES

IN THE UNITED STATES

M. LEONARD, INC.
241 Fox Drive
Piqua, OH 45356
Toll-free: (800) 543-8955
Website: www.amleo.com

BOUNTIFUL GARDENS
18001 Shafer Ranch Rd.
Willits, CA 95490-9626
Phone: (707) 459-6410
Website: www.bountifulgardens.org

FEDCO
P.O. Box 520-A
Waterville, ME 04903
Phone: (207) 873-7333
Fax: (207) 872-8317
Website: www.fedcoseeds.com

GARDENERS' SUPPLY COMPANY
128 Intervale Road
Burlington, VT 05401
Toll-free: (888) 833-1412
Website: www.gardeners.com

JOYNNY'S SELECTED SEEDS
184 Foss Hill Road
Albion, ME 04910
Phone: (207) 437-9294
Website: www.johnnyseeds.com

PEACEFUL VALLEY FARM SUPPLY
P.O. Box 2209
Grass Valley, CA 95945
Toll-free: (888) 784-1722
Website: www.groworganic.com

SEED SAVERS EXCHANGE
3076 North Winn Road
Decorah, IA 52101
(563) 382-5990
Website: www.seedsavers.org

WHITE FLOWER FARM
P.O. Box 50
Litchfield, CT 06759-0050
Toll-free: (800) 503-9624
Website: www.whiteflowerfarm.com

IN CANADA

RICHTERS
357 Highway 47
Goodwood, ON L0C 1A0
Phone: (905) 640-6677
Website: www.richters.com

VESEYS BULBS
P.O. Box 9000
Charlottetown, P.E. C1A 8K6
Website: www.veseys.com

WILLIAM DAM SEEDS
Box 8400
Dundas, ON l9H 6M1
Phone: (905) 628-6641
Website: www.damseeds.com

Index

Acknowledgments

The publisher wishes to thank all those who kindly supplied the photography for this book, as follows:

© **The National Magazine Company Limited** 1 (**Jacqui Hurst**), 3, 4-5 (**Clay Perry**), 6 (**Nicola Stocken Tomkins**), 7 (**Mark Bolton**), 10 (**Clay Perry**), 12 (right) (**Melanie Eclaire**), 13 (left) (**Jane Gifford**), 14 (**Andrew Lawson**), 15 (**Jacqui Hurst**), 26 (**Melanie Eclaire**), 27 (**Clay Perry**), 30-31 (**Clay Perry**), 37 (**John Glover**), 44-45 (**Jane Gifford**), 48-49 (**Jacqui Hurst**), 51 (**Jacqui Hurst**), 56 (left) (**Jacqui Hurst**), 56-57 (watermark) (**Clay Perry**), 57 (left) (**Melanie Eclaire**), 58-59 (**Stephen Robson**), 60 (right) (**Jacqui Hurst**), 61 (left) (**Jacqui Hurst**), 62 (**Jane Gifford**), 65 (top) (**Jane Gifford**), 68 (left) (**Jane Gifford**), 69 (right) (**Jacqui Hurst**), 70 (top) (**Michael Paul**), 70 (bottom) (**Kate Gadsby**), 72 (left and right) (**Adrian Briscoe**), 72 (middle) (**Jacqui Hurst**), 82 (left) (**Jacqui Hurst**), 82 (right) (**Nicola Stocken Tomkins**), 83 (right) (**Jacqui Hurst**), 88 (middle) (**Melanie Eclaire**), 93 (**Mark Bolton**), 94 (left) (**Kate Gadsby**), 94 (right) (**Stephen Robson**), 98 (**Jacqui Hurst**), 102 (**Clay Perry**), 108-109 (**Clay Perry**), 111 (bottom) (**Pia Tryde**), 113 (left) (**Andrea Jones**), 119 (**Huntley Hedworth**), 122-123 (**Mirjam Bleeker**), 132-133 (watermark) (**Stephen Robson**), 134 (**Spike Powell**), 135 (**Huntley Hedworth**), 136 (**Stephen Robson**), 144 (**Clay Perry**), 149 (**Hugo Burnand**), 151 (**Charlie Colmer**), 152 (right) (**Charlie Colmer**), 153 (**Jacqui Hurst**), 160 (left and right) (**Ian Skelton**), 161 (**David Ward**), 164 (left and middle) (**Pia Tryde**) and 165 (**Debbie Patterson**);

© **Steven Wooster** 2 (Nellie Hijmans Garden, Winssen, Holland), 11 (Yalding Garden), 12 (left), 13 (right) (Clonaveel, Jill Scott garden, Letterbreen, Enniskillen, Ireland), 18-19 (Nellie Hijmans Garden, Winssen, Holland), 28 (Boardman Garden, New Zealand; Boardman & Blackie Design), 32-33 (Denmans Garden), 34-35, 38-39 (Woodpeckers Garden), 40 ("Two Grahams Garden", New Zealand), 47 (Clonaveel, Jill Scott garden, Ireland), 50 (Clonaveel, Jill Scott garden, Ireland), 52, 54, 55 (top left) (Clonaveel, Jill Scott garden, Ireland), 55 (right) (Community-run organic vegetable garden, Auckland, New Zealand), 57 (right) (Clonaveel, Jill Scott garden, Ireland), 60 (left) (Broughton Castle), 61 (right), 78-79 (Nymans), 84 (left) (The Organic Centre, Rossinver, Co. Leitrim, Ireland), 89 (right) (Ayrlies, New Zealand), 91 (top), 91 (middle) (Château de Villandry), 91 (bottom) (Iford Manor), 103 (top and middle), 105 (middle), 106 (left and right), 111 (top) (Clonaveel, Jill Scott garden, Ireland), 113 (right) (Yalding Garden), 114 (left and right), 114 (middle) (Clonaveel, Jill Scott garden, Ireland), 117 (top, upper middle, lower middle and bottom), 120 (Clonaveel, Jill Scott garden, Ireland), 121 (top) (Wisley Garden), 121 (middle and bottom), 132 (left) (Hadspen House), 132 (right) (Four Aces Garden), 133 (right) (Woodstock Garden, Woodstock, South Island, New Zealand), 137 (top left) (Moss Green Garden, New Zealand), 137 (top right), 138 (Hadspen House), 142 (Four Aces Garden), 143 (The Old Rectory, Sudborough), 152 (left) (Sticky Wicket, Dorset) and 154-155 (Woodstock Garden, Woodstock, South Island, New Zealand);

© **J S Sira/Garden Picture Library** 8-9 and 129 (top);
© **Andrea Jones/Garden Exposures Photo Library** 12-13 (watermark), 42-43, 46 and 126;
© **Sunniva Harte/Garden Picture Library** 16-17;
© **Howard Rice/Garden Picture Library** 41, 86, 95 (right) and 124 (right);
© **John Daniels/Ardea** 53 (top);
© **Steve Hopkins/Ardea** 53 (upper middle);
© **Papilio/Ken Wilson** 53 (lower middle);
© **Ecoscene/Ian Beames** 53 (bottom);
Collins & Brown (Photographer: Steven Wooster) 55 (bottom left), 66 (left and right), 68 (right), 75 (left and right), 76, 80 (left), 103 (bottom), 105 (left), 105 (right) and 125 (top);
© **David Cavagnaro/Garden Picture Library** 56 (right), 80 (right) and 85;
Harry Smith Collection 65 (middle and bottom), 66 (middle), 69 (left), 75 (middle), 77 (top, middle and bottom), 83 (left), 88 (left) and 131 (top and middle);
Chrysalis Images 84 (right);
© **Lynn Brotchie/Garden Picture Library** 87;
© **John Beedle/Flowerphotos** 88 (right);
© **Brian Carter/Garden Picture Library** 89 (left);
© **Densey Clyne/Garden Picture Library** 95 (left);
© **Didier Willery/Garden Picture Library** 95 (middle);
© **John Glover/Garden Picture Library** 99 (top), 100 (left), 127, 137 (bottom) and 166;
© **Mark Bolton/Garden Picture Library** 99 (middle) and 124 (left);
© **Andrea Jones/Garden Picture Library** 99 (bottom);
© **Chris Burrows/Garden Picture Library** 100 (right);
© **Peter Gasson/Wild Images/RSPCA Photolibrary** 101;
© **Mel Watson/Garden Picture Library** 125 (middle);
© **Jonathan Plant/RSPCA Photolibrary** 125 (bottom);
© **Linda Burgess (Gardens/Plants)/Garden Picture Library** 129 (middle);
© **Clive Nichols/Garden Picture Library** 128, 129 (bottom);
© **Kevin Richardson/Garden Picture Library** 131 (bottom);
© **Brigitte Thomas/Garden Picture Library** 133 (left) and 147;
© **Eric Crichton/Garden Picture Library** 97, 140 and 141;
© **Stuart Harrop/RSPCA Photolibrary** 139;
© **Ron Sutherland/Garden Picture Library** 146;
© **Mayer/Le Scanff/Garden Picture Library** 150 and 156-157;
© **Juliette Wade/Garden Picture Library** 159;
© **Ecoscene/Tony Page** 162;
© **Chris Knights/Ardea** 164 (right).

A Zone Map of the U.S. and Canada

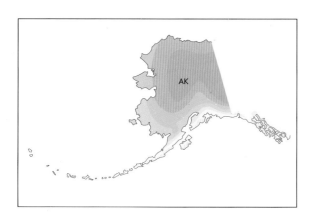

A plant's winter hardiness is critical in deciding whether it is suitable for your garden. The map below divides the United States and Canada into 11 climactic zones based on average minimum temperatures, as compiled by the U.S. Department of Agriculture. Find your zone and check the zone information in the plant directory to help you choose the plants most likely to flourish in your climate.

		Fahrenheit	Celsius
Zone 1		below -50°	below -46°
Zone 2		-50° to -40°	-46° to -40°
Zone 3		-40° to -30°	-40° to -34°
Zone 4		-30° to -20°	-34° to -29°
Zone 5		-20° to -10°	-29° to -23°
Zone 6		-10° to 0°	-23° to -18°
Zone 7		0° to 10°	-18° to -12°
Zone 8		10° to 20°	-12° to -7°
Zone 9		20° to 30°	-7° to -1°
Zone 10		30° to 40°	-1° to 4°
Zone 11		above 40°	above 4°